Mary
SLESSOR

LIGHT FOR THE DARK CONTINENT

SAM WELLMAN

BARBOUR
PUBLISHING

Mary
SLESSOR

Cover illustration © Dick Bobnick
Cover design by Douglas Miller (mhpubarts.com)

Published by Barbour Publishing, Inc., P.O. Box 719, Uhrichsville, OH 44683, www.barbourbooks.com

Our mission is to publish and distribute inspirational products offering exceptional value and biblical encouragement to the masses.

 Member of the
Evangelical Christian
Publishers Association

Printed in the United States of America.
5 4 3 2 1

*To the pure hearts who have gone to
"teach all nations, baptizing them
in the name of the Father,
and of the Son,
and of the Holy Ghost."*

ONE

Mary Mitchell Slessor's heart thumped within her. "Oh no, Reverend. I couldn't do that."

"But why, Miss Slessor?" asked the pastor. "You speak to the children all the time. I've heard you. You know the scriptures well. Surely you won't mind going up on the platform and speaking to the adults of our fellowship on 'The common people heard Him gladly.' "

Mary glanced shyly around the meeting hall. No one had heard the pastor's words to her. Good. "Perhaps I may speak to them just as I am, Reverend? I mean right here. To as few as want to listen."

So on the floor of the meeting hall that February night of 1874 Mary spoke to people gathered around—consciously avoiding eye contact with men. She elaborated on the twelfth chapter of Mark and how Jesus was confronted first by the learned Pharisees and next by the aristocratic Sadducees before once again He and His good news were received with joy by the common people.

"Very well explained, Mary," enthused the pastor.

"I'm only repeating that which I read in the Gospel," said Mary, anxious to leave the hall.

And leave the hall she soon did. She scurried toward home. There were few about in the dark winter-chilled streets of Dundee, Scotland, but the few who were about were known well enough by her to worry her.

She still ached from her refusal to speak from the platform. She could scarcely explain her self-consciousness. At twenty-five she was short but solid, with a pleasant, soft-freckled face. Her long, thick hair flamed vermilion. But she carried her dead father's shame to be sure. Who was she to rise above the others to speak? How many Saturday nights had she waited with her mother in the cold grip of dread before her father stumbled in, bleary-eyed and slurring his words? As often as not, the drunken fool had hurled his meal, cold but much needed by the children, into the fireplace. Mother had rebuked his selfishness.

Once in a while Mary, too, had condemned him. A reprimand from offspring he would not tolerate. He had raged against Mary so violently she had escaped into the dark cobbled streets.

Even now, remembering his abandoned shoemaker's tools and leather-soaking sink made Mary tremble with fear and anger. Yes, that pitiful man, dead but never forgotten, was her heritage.

"And, O Lord, how I wanted to be like Dr. Livingstone," she sighed as she rushed home.

The great Scottish missionary David Livingstone was Mary's hero. She'd read *Missionary Travels*, hardly stopping to breathe. A second time. A third time. He was a Scot, just like her. He was the second oldest of seven children, just like her. He had been poor, just like her. He had even worked in a textile mill many years, just like her! How many times had she told herself, *Then cannot I be a missionary just like him? Yes, to Africa just like Livingstone.*

But then how many times had her heart ached when she remembered what a godly father Livingstone sprang from? His father presented him from infancy with a "consistent example of piety" so priestly, Livingstone claimed, that his father could best be depicted only by the father Bobby Burns described poetically in "The Cotter's Saturday Night." Unfortunately, Mary remembered every stanza Burns composed about that Bible-living patriarch, including the conclusion.

" 'From scenes like these, old Scotia's grandeur springs,' " recited Mary with pain.

Her own late father had been a Saturday-night monster. Oh, the shame she carried. She tried to forgive him. At times she was sure she had forgiven him. But then, like tonight, she realized the hate, the resentment, the fears, still gnawed inside her.

She could mount no platform to speak. Not carrying his shame on her small shoulders like heavy chains. Because of her father's transgressions, the family had left their cottage on the sunny, green outskirts of Aberdeen to come to the dank, grimy slums of Dundee. Left behind was Mother's beloved Belmont Street church.

All was changed, turned topsy-turvy, so Father might have a second chance. It was his last. He drank himself into a grave, but not before his money-hungry habit had helped drive four of Mary's food- and sun-starved siblings into their graves. Only Mary and her two younger sisters, Susan and Jane, were still alive.

"God forgive the monster. But so must I!" she muttered, remembering scripture. "Praise God, Mother found the church for us here in Dundee, too."

She entered a turret at the end of a grim tenement building and skipped up the spiral staircase. She rushed down a landing, never doubting for a moment a certain window would have a candle glowing to welcome her home.

"Mother!" she said gratefully as she breezed into the tiny one-room apartment. But her voice was as soft as a dove's wings because her two sisters lay asleep on a trundle bed on the floor.

"How was fellowship?" asked mother.

"Very nice." Mary sat on the floor next to Mother's rocking chair.

"Did you have any missionaries there?"

"Not tonight, Mother."

"Seems awhile since we've heard of Calabar."

"Oh, you and your Calabar in west Africa!" Mary teased, but in a voice barely above a whisper.

"And yours too, child."

"Besides, we read every month of their doings in the *Missionary Record*," reminded Mary.

"Yes, but occasionally one of the saints comes home on furlough." Mother added excitedly, "Don't you remember Reverend Anderson of Calabar?"

"Of course, Mother."

It seemed to Mary she had lived in Calabar longer than Dundee. Her church, the United Presbyterian Church of Scotland, once called the Secession Church, had been in on the mission at Calabar from the beginning.

Reverend Hope Waddell started it in 1846 with a group of freed Jamaican slaves who originally came from that part of west Africa. Calabar was the name of a region around the Calabar and Cross rivers. But the name also came to mean the missionaries' first station on "Mission Hill" above a village called Duke Town. The industrious missionaries had added missions at Old Town, Creek Town, Eknetu, and Okofiorong—all upriver from the first station. Mary knew full well the missions were now manned by five ordained missionaries, helped by a dozen or so men and women lay teachers.

"No talk of missions tonight, then?" asked mother uneasily.

"That's the second time you've asked me," replied Mary suspiciously. "You are not telling me something, Mother. And it must be something you do not wish to tell me yourself. What is it? Are the missionaries having trouble at Calabar? Did one of the native chiefs die?"

"No. . ."

"You must tell me."

"I heard some people say Dr. Livingstone is dead."

"No!"

The thought of Dr. Livingstone dead tore at Mary's heart. That good man and his great work in Africa finished? Who could replace Livingstone? Not ten missionaries. Not one hundred.

But wait. Hadn't the newspapers reported his death before? And hadn't some American journalist gone down into east Africa and found him alive and well at Ujiji? Mary must not panic.

"You are taking it better than I thought you would," said Mother quietly.

"The story may not be true."

"They say some natives brought his body to the east coast of Africa, and a ship is bringing his body back to London, where he will be buried at Westminster Abbey."

"Doctor Livingstone has very powerful friends in London's scientific community," reasoned Mary. "Surely they will determine if the remains are really those of the good doctor."

It was weeks later—in the month of April—that a report in a newspaper broke the news.

TWO

No!" cried Mary.

At first she wanted to throw the newspaper aside and scream, "No, you mustn't bury this corpse you falsely call Livingstone!" but then she saw the proof. The newspaper detailed how a distinguished surgeon had examined the corpse. He determined the left upper arm bone of the corpse had a severe fracture that had never mended. Mary knew from Livingstone's own writings that he had been maimed by the jaws of a lion in that exact spot. His left arm had a false joint between shoulder and elbow. Imagine! In the jaws of a lion. All to serve Christ. The terrible stinking fangs of a lion. And what had she, Mary Mitchell Slessor, done?

"I don't care *where* we go as long as we go *forward*!" she cried, remembering Livingstone's famous words.

Forward! Yes, she had hesitated long enough. She must go forward. For thirteen years Mary had labored full-time in the mill, bringing home money for food and shelter. She was proficient. She was now running not one but two looms, weaving hour after hour without pause like a hot, laboring machine herself. But enough was enough. Her two sisters, even young Jane at fourteen, were old enough now to help Mother. Mary must go forward to serve Christ. In the next weeks, in her hours away from the looms, she would seek advice: Should she volunteer for missionary work or not?

One of the first she asked was an old friend. It had been a widow—God bless the dear woman's nosiness—who had seen Mary at no more than eleven years old running the slum streets with a gang of other dirty children. It had been a wintry day that bit Mary's skin with needle teeth, or Mary would never have accepted the widow's invitation to come inside her lodgings. But the warmth of the fire had drawn her—and it had been the fire that changed Mary.

"Do you see that fire?" the widow had demanded. "If you put your hand in that fire, it would sear you with unbearable pain. If you don't repent of your sins and accept the Lord Jesus Christ as your Savior, your soul will burn in a hellfire just like that—forever and ever!"

Mary trembled with dread.

Then the widow went on to soothe her with words from the Bible. Repent. Accept Christ as her Savior. Mary's mother read the Bible to her too, but it was that widow who convinced Mary to her very core of the perils of sin. The widow's warning branded Mary. The fear of hell filled Mary with dread. Over the years that feeling never went away.

"Do you think a woman like me should go to a far-off country to do missionary work among the savages?"

Mary asked her old friend.

"Pray and be silent, lassie," advised the widow. "Listen hard for God's answer."

So Mary did pray hard and listen. And it did seem God was speaking to her. Didn't she read the holy scripture and try to live by God's words? So it was not surprising that in Mary's long silence her mind was drawn to scripture. Wasn't this God's way of talking to her? Her mind was drawn to the Great Commission expressed by Christ himself in Matthew 28:19:

> *Go ye therefore, and teach all nations,*
> *baptizing them in the name of the Father,*
> *and of the Son, and of the Holy Ghost. . . .*

That was plain enough. The Lord wanted His disciples to go forth to all the nations. But Mary also thought of Saint Paul's words in verses 11 and 12 of Ephesians 4:

> *And He gave some, apostles; and some,*
> *prophets; and some, evangelists; and some,*
> *pastors and teachers; for the perfecting of*
> *the saints, for the work of the ministry, for*
> *the edifying of the body of Christ.*

Of course. Not every disciple could go to other nations, or who would serve the flock at home? So Mary continued to ask people for advice, as she prayed.

One of the next she asked was an old adversary. "What do you think of a woman like me going to a far-off country to do missionary work among the savages?"

"You would ask me such an important question?" the young man blurted in astonishment. "I thought you disliked me."

"Not at all. I love you like a brother. But I ask you because you are also a leader. Give me advice."

He was the very gang leader who as a boy challenged Mary before a youth meeting. He twirled a lead weight at the end of a string closer and closer to her. It was a wrong-headed brattish stunt to scare and humiliate her. But the surly look in his eyes changed into confusion and fear as the weight whirred closer and closer to her face and she would not move. Finally the weight grazed her forehead. He dropped the weight, shamed by his own cruelty, his own sinfulness. Her will had crushed his will. He motioned his gang to follow him and slouched into the youth meeting.

"I pity those poor savages," he said to Mary this day.

She consulted another tough she had faced down. This boy, now a man, had stood outside her meeting with a whip. He enjoyed lashing boys, driving them into her meeting, pretending to help her but actually discouraging them from ever showing up again. Naturally he refused to come inside himself.

One day, with no warning to herself, Mary confronted him. "What would happen if we changed places?" she asked.

"Why, I'd get this whip across my back!" he snorted.

"Not at all," she replied. "In fact, I'll gladly bear a whip lashing from you right now if you will go inside to the meeting." She turned her back to him.

"Would you really?" he cried, his voice suddenly choking.

"Do it," she said, "as hard and as often as you like." He threw the whip down and walked inside.

That convert said to her this day, "I can't imagine anyone stopping you. Or wanting to."

But not all encouraged her. Some in the church begged her not to do it. Didn't she know these far-off tropical countries were the white person's grave? Many missionaries died in their first years there. Mosquito nets, pith helmets, boiled water, and quinine could not save them. They died anyway. Thus, Mary was warned by these well-meaning discouragers who had probably seen her pale with fear if asked to speak. How could they know why she felt so unworthy in such circumstances? How could they know she faced physical dangers with God-blessed assurance?

Some in the church encouraged her. Older friends like James Logie told her to forge ahead. God would guide her. Mary did not have to ask her mother. *The day I volunteer for missionary service, Mother will be both the saddest and happiest woman in Scotland*, Mary told herself.

One night as she lay in bed, immersed in silence, she had an inspiration. "God, speak to my heart," she prayed, "and in Your mercy and loving kindness, don't let me be tricked by the devil!" So she thought very hard of staying in Dundee, working at the mill but also helping the local church. Her heart warmed to the notion. Then she thought very hard of sitting in a village of thatch-roofed huts, teaching small children. Whether the babes were Oriental or black she couldn't tell. But her heart warmed to that notion too. Suddenly in her thoughts a child toddled forward, black arms outstretched, black cheeks stained with tears. Mary clutched the black baby to her heart. Mary seemed transported into the heavens.

What unutterable joy! I must read and reread the issues of the Missionary Record, she counseled herself, hardly able to sleep. *After all, I must decide what country in Africa beckons me.*

Her church was active in India, China, Japan, and Africa. In Africa, missions were established in Calabar in west Africa and in Kaffir Land in south Africa. The Kaffirs were also called Zulus. Missionary work in Kaffir Land would bring Mary right into contact with the early work of her hero, Livingstone, among the neighboring Bechuanas. So, occasionally she thought of serving these tall, red-blanketed Kaffirs. But somehow she seemed always drawn to Calabar. Was God telling her to go to Calabar? It would surely please Mother.

It was James Logie who pushed her the final few steps. Since she sought his advice, he had become a member of the Foreign Mission Board. "Why do you hesitate, Mary?" he asked her. "If you wish I'll look in on your family here. The mission board won't let them want for any necessities."

Mary gulped. "Then it's forward, Mr. Logie."

Yet she still did not apply to the board, because one evening while talking quietly with mother she was overcome with guilt and shame. Was she going to wound her mother as her father had? She had allowed herself to think of Mother's home in Old Meldrum. Yes, Mother was once the only child of pious tradesmen, a child educated, well-dressed, and refined. Dear Mother was a privileged child. She lived in a gentle land of sparkling streams and treeless heath, timid rabbits and furtive salmon. How Mother's heart must have ached when her groom, a young shoemaker from Buchan, took her away to Gilcomston, a suburb of Aberdeen. Still, they had lived in their beloved Highlands. But later, oh how Mother must have cried when they moved to Dundee and the Lowlands. And to the slums. Yet, Mother did not openly complain except against his drinking. How much harder it must be for one who has had a taste of the peaceful, pastoral life of the Highlands to barely survive in the slums of a factory city. Could Mary leave her mother now? Wouldn't her departure be just one more thorn in her mother's side?

"You must go to Calabar," said her mother one evening several weeks later.

"Calabar? We haven't talked about Calabar in ages."

"I know. You avoid it." Her mother held her hand. "Once, I thought your older brother Robert would go to Calabar. Remember how he said he would take you with him? But poor Robert died, a mere lad of sixteen. God had other plans for him. Then I was sure God wanted your brother John to go to Calabar. But God took him too."

"But Mother," interrupted Mary, "if you were so sure about Robert and John going to Calabar, yet wrong, how can you be sure about me going to Calabar?"

"Oh, you stubborn lass," teased Mother, "of course I don't know for sure. But if I thought you would not go serve Christ in order to spare my feelings I would be heartbroken to the very end of my days."

But then Mary did a very strange thing, whether impulse or a nudge from God she could not tell. When she applied to the Foreign Mission Board she told them she would go wherever she was needed. It was as if she had to tell God "Yes, I have decided on Calabar in what may be my own stumbling way, but now I realize You must decide, Lord. Now I will know for sure Your will for me." Even more frightful to Mary was increasing worry that she would be turned down for any foreign assignment. For after all, she was not educated. She was a mere factory lass—a tiny lass at that—with no special talents other than weaving. Still, when at last Mary was summoned to the Foreign Mission Board, she was not fearful.

" 'For God hath not given us the spirit of fear; but of power, and of love, and of a sound mind,' " she reminded herself. "But I am very nervous," she admitted.

And why not? After all, her future—the fulfillment or denial of her dreams, yes, even her mother's dreams—would soon be revealed to her.

THREE

S it down, Miss Slessor," said one of the commissioners as Mary entered the meeting room of the Foreign Mission Board.

Mary was pleased to see James Logie among the men. "Thank you," she replied quietly.

"Your application to the board is timely," said one of the commissioners. "Calabar has requested more teachers."

"Calabar!" gasped Mary.

She thanked the commissioners and left, her mind reeling. Was it possible after so many years of dreaming and wondering? Yes, she had the dream in her grasp, and she must not let go. In the following days her mother reassured her over and over that far from being a hardship for her it fulfilled her dreams too. How her mother longed to read the *Missionary Record* and see the name of her own dear child working for Christ.

"To read 'the missionary Mary Slessor,'" enthused Mother. "Imagine!"

It did seem to compensate for all the hardship, all the disappointments. It was not long before Mary left for Edinburgh to receive training for her assignment. Mary was dazzled. Wide avenues like Princes Street were lined with shops. High above Edinburgh sat a castle, ancient and massive. Scattered throughout the city were towering Gothic spires of churches. Grimy Dundee was not like this. Edinburgh seemed truly the pure heart of Scotland. How lucky Mary felt to be there at long last.

Edinburgh was astir with church activity. The American evangelist D. L. Moody had recently held a great revival there. Mary had been aware he had spoken in Forfar, too, about a five-hour walk north of Dundee, but any kind of travel for the impoverished Slessors had been out of the question. So Moody had brought his revival to Mary's part of Scotland, too, before he went back to America, but she had been little affected.

"Edinburgh is still quite wrapped up in Moody's revival movement," said her Edinburgh host, Robert Martin, who was very active in the Bristo Street congregation of the church. "There seem to be few who didn't hear him preach."

"I wish I could have heard him," said Mary politely.

"A most loving and wise man, once you got used to his coarse, American way of speaking," said her host. "And he had a wonderful singer with him, a Mr. Ira Sankey."

Mary was far more interested in another visitor to Edinburgh. "And did you hear Dr. Livingstone, sir?"

"Good heavens, Livingstone?" he replied. "His visit was nearly twenty years ago."

"Then you did hear him?" pressed Mary excitedly.

"Yesss. . . ," Robert Martin drawled as he frowned back the memory. His face brightened. "The year was 1857. Dr. Livingstone was wiry and very fit. His clothing seemed cut for a heavier man. Anyway, his attire was indifferent—and out-of-date at that. His face was dark and deeply wrinkled. He was quite foreign looking. Thoroughly Africanized, I suppose. He spoke with a most peculiar accent, too—Scottish and yet foreign—and in short bursts. Often he wrestled for a word. Sometimes he could not complete a sentence because he failed to find the right word. He apologized, explaining he had not spoken English in sixteen years. His narrative skipped about freely, too. But his message was so powerful that it overcame his faltering tongue. And the message was quite clear: Africa must be opened up for Christ!"

"Were you stirred then by his message?" asked Mary.

"Frankly, I recall that I was a bit disappointed at the time. But my memory of him is very strong, so surely Christ worked through him.

" 'Well, I have begun the work,' Dr. Livingstone suddenly snapped at the conclusion of his talk, 'and I go back to carry on!' His ending implied, 'And what are *you* going to do?' He gave three talks, I believe. In spite of his language difficulty the conscience of Edinburgh was quite strongly affected, which it proved later by sponsoring the Livingstonia Mission in Nyasaland."

"Wonderful," gushed Mary.

Over the next weeks Mary pressed Mr. Martin and others for other anecdotes of the great man. There were many. Some sounded apocryphal, but some sounded characteristic of Livingstone. At a breakfast in Edinburgh one well-meaning cleric suggested sponsoring a pension for Livingstone, which triggered a very sour look from the missionary. Pension? Retire? Livingstone could be sharper and more direct than a sour look. To any armchair traveler who self-righteously questioned his methods he could be blunt, snapping, "My ideal of a missionary isn't so narrow as a dumpy man with a Bible under his arm; my ideal is carrying a hammer and a saw!" Mary's heart was warmed by anecdotes of Livingstone that sounded true. It made her decision to be a missionary seem a certain step in the right direction.

"Dr. Livingstone is my exemplar of a missionary," she confided in Mr. Martin's unmarried daughter who still lived at home.

Mary became good friends with Mr. Martin's married daughter, Mrs. M'Crindle, too. They all participated in the Bristo Street church activities. But Mary's main purpose in Edinburgh was to absorb schooling at the Canongate Normal School. Students there certainly took note of the fact that Mary was going to Calabar. A few tried to scare her. She expected it. No one knew better than she how her tiny frame and freckled face drew assumptions of vulnerability. Didn't she know the natives around Calabar were cannibals? insisted her antagonists. Didn't she know the heathen of Africa worshipped the devil? And what of the ferocious leopards that lurked behind every tree?

"Well, if it's the post of danger, then it is surely also the post of honor," she countered.

But the thought of a leopard did frighten her, more than the thought of heathens. After all, one could not evangelize a hungry beast! She knew nothing about the animal called a leopard except that holy scripture mentioned it several times as a fierce spotted beast, usually in the same breath with a lion or a wolf. Did Calabar really have leopards? She had to learn more about Calabar. So, between Normal School and the real missionaries she met occasionally in Edinburgh, she began to learn much about the real Calabar. Thanks to Prince Henry of Portugal, west Africa had been known to Europeans since the 1430s. Henry simply sent the old caravels on repeated voyages from Portugal to extend European knowledge of the African coastline ever farther southward. European royalty were motivated by many reasons, good and bad. They desired knowledge. They wished to spread Christianity.

"But they also wanted to find wealth," admitted Mary.

Soon the Portuguese had staked a chain of trading settlements along the west coast of Africa. Gold and ivory were exploited by trading posts, but the plunder was meager compared to that from the Americas. Great wealth was not realized in Africa until the Americas began importing black slaves from there. Then the entire west coast of Africa festered with slave trading. Battles for control over this new commerce intensified. A great sea power like Britain soon dominated the trade. Millions of Africans were captured by other Africans and exchanged for ironware, firearms, and fabric. But sentiment mounted against the slave trade. By 1807 the British Parliament outlawed the slave trade for British citizens. The British navy began actively opposing slave trade.

"There is nothing quite like the sight of dozens of

yawning cannons on a great warship to cause repentance in the hardest of sinners," reasoned Mary.

But good Christians were interested in Africa, too. To their credit their missionaries were soon there on many fronts. The CMS of London, the Methodists, and the Baptists were in several coastal areas. Mary's own Presbyterians were in the Calabar region of the coast. Though slavery greatly diminished, other commerce developed. The industrial revolution, powered by machines—as Mary well knew—had been long under way. And in west Africa the British found an inexhaustible and cheap supply of superb machine oil.

"Palm oil," said Mary in wonder, "extracted from the husk of a palm fruit."

"The palm-oil trees top out at 60 feet," explained a veteran missionary of Calabar. "They must be climbed to harvest the fruit. The climber hacks the leaves away with a machete and lowers 50-pound clusters of the fruit with a rope. The fruits are bright red and tinged a bit black as if scorched. A mature tree can yield 600 pounds of fruit at a picking. Mind you, the natives must be discouraged from draining sap from the trunk of the palm to make their wine. That lowers the yield of fruit." He paused to add distastefully, "That is more or less how our government justifies sending the natives rum and gin. . . ."

"Rum and gin!" objected Mary.

"The husk of the fruit is boiled," continued the missionary uncomfortably. "It yields the oil. If the nut inside the hull is cracked it surrenders a kernel that also yields oil but with much more difficulty. It has become customary for the natives to simply export the kernels to

Britain so they can be crushed by massive machines."

"Rum and gin?" repeated Mary, still dismayed.

"The palm oil can be used for much more than machine oil," interrupted the missionary brightly. "The better grades are used for cooking oil and the lesser grades for candles and soap."

So Mary learned that after the slave trade was outlawed the British were still interested in the area for palm oil. Britain's direct influence ashore began in 1849 under the consulship of John Beecroft. His efforts were not simple diplomacy, but what came to be called "gunboat diplomacy." In 1852 he forced out the ruler of Lagos, west of the Niger delta, and pressured his successor, King Akitoye, to accept British protection. Nine years later the British annexed Lagos as a crown colony. Beecroft's successor, Consul Lynslager, was just as heavy-handed.

Mary now realized the force that Britain used to stop slavery had also been used for oppression. To her dismay she learned none other than David Livingstone's late brother Charles had been such a consul of Calabar once.

Disappointed but undaunted, Mary asked the missionary, "And what of the natives, Reverend?"

"It's a most peculiar situation," he mulled, "not that the peculiar is unusual for Africa. The natives we deal with are the Efiks. They have a long history of being middlemen, so to speak, between the British and the tribes farther inland: the Okoyong, Ibo, and Ibibio. The Efiks are governed by clans, much like we Scots once were. Each clan is basically one village run by a chief, which the British magnanimously call a 'king.' " He hesitated.

"What is it, Reverend?'

"Well, it is so complicated. . . ."

"But I thought they were simple pagans with simple beliefs. . . ."

"Oh no, lassie. There is nothing simple about them. You see, the clans are made up of both freemen and slaves. And there is a secret organization of freemen that operates outside the clan system. These are the Egbos. Vigilantes. In disguise, they confront wrongdoers directly and administer what they consider justice—often quite violent justice. On the other hand there is a secret organization of slaves called the Blood Men who try to punish those who are too unjust to the slaves. . . ." He stopped, frowning.

"Please go on, Reverend."

"Well, it might be better if you discovered these things for yourself. I'm afraid I will only confuse you. Perhaps I'm a little confused myself. Some say the Blood Men were put down. And some say there is a new secret society called the Leopard Men. . . ."

"And what about our mission schools, Reverend? Are the poor slaves not allowed to attend?"

He laughed nervously. "In fact, the slave boys are about the only ones who do attend. School is considered too much a hardship for a freeman."

Mary blinked in disbelief. "I see that it is very complicated. . . ."

"I can tell you something of the language of the Efiks. It is difficult for us Scots because it is tonal. The same word might mean different things depending on the pitch. For example, the very same word could mean 'chicken' or 'millstone' or 'knife,' depending on whether the pitch is low, medium, or high!"

Mary held up her hand. "Perhaps it is too early for me to be thinking about the language, Reverend."

She didn't tell the missionary that she planned on learning the language directly from the natives' mouths, never from a book. Her hero David Livingstone had done just that very thing. He had gone off from the mission at Kuruman to live with the Bakwains until he was fluent in Bechuana. In fact, if she was not mistaken, Livingstone was twenty-nine when he mastered Bechuana. Mary was not yet twenty-eight! Over the weeks Mary's zeal became so great and so contagious that Mr. Martin's unmarried daughter and her close friend decided they, too, would apply to become missionaries. At first Mary doubted them. Yet the two did apply to the board, not to go to Africa but to China.

In the summer of 1876 Mary's preparation for Calabar was deemed complete. She was allowed to return to Dundee to say her farewells. To her relief, her family seemed to be faring quite well without her. But why shouldn't they? Wasn't Mother's health all right? Wasn't sister Susan a grown woman now? Wasn't the "baby sister," Jane, now an almost-grown lass at sixteen? And after all, hadn't Mary herself worked full-time in the mills since the age of twelve? Why should she fret so for her mother and sisters? Mary must now serve the Master. Indeed at the final farewell, doubt suddenly thrust itself on her own future.

"Oh please, pray for me!" she urged her mother and sisters.

Then Mary journeyed to Liverpool with two men from the mission board. The 200-mile train ride to

Liverpool alone seemed the trip of a lifetime to Mary. From the undulating heath of Scotland the train rolled into the ever more verdant pastures of England, with ever more rivers and woodlands. Mary never knew nature could produce such rich shades of green. Great rivers, roiling browns and tans, carried rich spoils never seen in Scotland. Finally, the three left the train and rode by coach to the docks.

"Where is the *Pearl*?" asked Mary, bewildered by the thicket of masts in the harbor.

"The *Pearl*?" asked her companions in astonishment. "Directly before us is your vessel, the steamer *Ethiopia*."

"Oh, I meant the *Ethiopia*, of course," said Mary, too embarrassed to explain that the *Pearl* left Liverpool for Africa in 1858, carrying David Livingstone! But she really felt more than ever she was following the footsteps of her hero.

"What are they loading?" she asked, anxious to change the subject. Neat stacks of kegs and cartons were being hoisted aboard the *Ethiopia* and lowered into the hold. She suggested optimistically, "Kegs of nails and boxes of Bibles?"

"No, my dear lady," said one of her companions in a sad voice. "The ship's main cargo is woe, sorrow, contentions, babbling, wounds, and redness of eyes."

The daughter of a drunkard easily recognized his allusion. Mary quoted Proverbs 23:29, "Who hath woe? who hath sorrow? who hath contentions? who hath babbling? who hath wounds without cause? who hath redness of eyes?"

"Yes, dear lass," said her companion. "The kegs are

filled with rum; the cartons contain bottles of gin."

"Lord help us," she gasped. "All that sinfulness and just one tiny missionary?"

The "one tiny missionary" sailed from England on the steamer *Ethiopia* on Saturday, August 5, 1876.

FOUR

"Miss Mary Slessor, welcome aboard," greeted the captain of the *Ethiopia*.

She had her own cabin, so small that both the bunk and the washbasin folded down from the wall—but to her it was luxurious. Seemingly oblivious to their evil cargo of liquor, the captain and crew were kind to her. And she had godly traveling companions in Mr. Thomson and his wife, a couple that intended to go beyond the coastal lowlands of Calabar to the Cameroon Mountains.

The next day, the Lord's Day without a church service, would have distressed Mary if she had not been so seasick. But the great swells of the Irish Sea were too much for a lass who had never ridden anything rougher than choppy waves on a ferry boat. She felt even worse as they passed the southern tip of England, ominously called "Land's End."

But several days later she was bubbly Mary again.

"Praise God, the sickness is over."

The *Ethiopia* was a steamer but under sail scudded easily south in the strong trade winds of summer. Steam power was saved for headwinds and surging river currents. The 5,000-mile trip seemed almost as impossible to Mary as a trip to the moon, but a steady 10 miles per hour inexorably pulled her closer and closer to her destination. In just one week the *Ethiopia* lay somewhere off an unseen northwest Africa. Mary found herself more and more often on deck, looking east across the rolling blue-green vastness.

"Land ahoy!" yelled a sailor one day.

But it was much too soon for Calabar. The sailor had spotted Cape Verde, the westernmost point of all Africa. It was also the site of the city of Dakar, but the *Ethiopia* would not put ashore there. It sailed on. The sea was smoother now, and often Mary could see a distant white glimmer on the eastern horizon. She was told those were beaches of white sand. One day the *Ethiopia* no longer scudded south but plowed east, often under steam power. The distant shores were now on the northern horizon. The air now carried not only a salty fishy smell but a spicy smell too. Yes, it was some exotic sample wafting from Africa. What the spice was Mary could not know. Finally one day a green mountain grew out of the glassy sea.

"Sierra Leone," announced a sailor with pleasure.

Mary began to discern neat white houses on the mountainside. As the *Ethiopia* neared Sierra Leone, small canoes the crew called "bumboats" approached. In them were blacks dressed in very bright fabrics. They were selling and buying. From the rail she watched with curiosity. Her ears longed for the voices of Africa. But both crew and natives spoke a coarse pidgin English.

Mary did not venture ashore until they anchored in Bonny many days farther east. This port was close now to Efik country, according to Mr. Thomson. In a sense it was Efik, he said. The area was dominated by Chief Jaja, originally an Ibo but also an exslave of one of the Efik clans.

"My first step on Africa," she said as a sailor from the ship helped her step out of the skiff onto white sand.

Beyond the beach the vegetation was lush, topped by swaying palm trees. The sailor led Mary into the bush, past whitewashed mud huts and into a market-place. The air was warm and heavy. Yes, this was truly Africa. Many goats were tethered in the market. Neat piles of food were being sold there too. She recognized ears of corn, peppers, and several kinds of bananas but little else.

"Them things would be cocoyams," explained the sailor, pointing to a pile of dusky tubers. "Them's man-ioc," he said, gesturing to larger tubers. "Them's yams." He pointed at orangish tubers that looked familiar to Mary. "A nice English lady like you won't be wanting any of that tucker," insisted the sailor.

"Good boiled beef and suet pudding for us, right?" said Mary agreeably, but as soon as it was convenient she planned on eating the African fare just the same. "What would be in the clay jars?"

"Palm oil," said the sailor.

"Of course," she realized, then was startled by the sight of a very large, very repulsive lizard ambling though the marketplace. "What is that?"

"Blimey," said the sailor, "it must be six or seven feet long. It's a monitor lizard. These heathen worship it. It's got the run of the place like them cows over in India."

"What a frightfully snakey beast."

"That little beastie would be lunch for the crocodiles around Calabar, lady."

Soon Mary was back on the *Ethiopia*, the ship once again steaming east. It was Mr. Thomson who pointed out the next day that a mountain looming far in the distance was his destination: Mount Cameroon. Near black rocks jutting out of the foaming sea the steamer turned north. Then the sea became a sheet of glass, no longer blue-green but brownish green, then brown. Then an enigma!

"I see distant shorelines on both sides of the *Ethiopia*," she blurted to Thomson. "How can that be?"

"We've turned up the Cross River. The mouth of the river is ten miles wide here."

"Ten miles wide!"

The river narrowed as they plowed upstream. Mary was told both banks were dense mangrove forests. The great mangrove trees flourished in the shallow fringes of the river. She was warned these fetid swampy fringes were also the favorite haunts of massive crocodiles.

Surely the horrid reptiles could not be as large as the sailors claimed, worried Mary.

River traffic began to appear. "A shrimper," a sailor explained as a low sloop of a boat drifted past, carrying nets.

The air was very heavy. "But it's not hot here," she said in amazement.

More and more islands emerged from the river,

seeming to make the river ever smaller. The channel shrank until Mary could now clearly see the banks on either side. The pale fluted mangrove trunks were vivid now. So were parrots, swooping down off the limbs, fluttering bright greens and reds and blues. A monkey! Several. The trees were alive with animals.

"Look there, lady," said a sailor pointing to a mud-bank in the trees.

Crocodile! The sailors had been right. How long was the dingy gray dragon? Twenty feet? How heavy? Half a ton? Immobile, it must have been sleeping. Its sides bulged. The legs seemed mere decoration. Perhaps they moved ever so slowly like a turtle. *Or better yet, a snail,* hoped Mary.

"Surely such a large beast is very slow," she suggested to the sailor.

"They drift as motionless as old logs in the river right up to the shore." The sailor's voice thinned in genuine fear. "Then they launch themselves out of the water at their poor victims. They strike like lightning."

"Lord help us," she gasped.

"I'm sorry, lady, but you need to know. In one gulp such a beast would chomp you in its jaws and yank you back in the river."

What was God's purpose of such terror in nature? It was a mystery—one more—not to be understood by mere mortals.

The *Ethiopia* turned hard to the right.

Mary heard a sailor mutter without looking up from his work, "We turned hard to starboard, mates, so we've entered the Calabar River."

The Thomsons joined her at the rail. Soon an

embankment rose from the foliage on the right. It was blanketed by green, so dense Mary couldn't tell whether the growth was ten feet tall or one hundred feet tall.

Thomson seemed awed. "We've left the mangrove swamps. This is real jungle now."

About an hour later drab huts materialized in the distance. "That would be Old Town," commented Thomson.

"But I thought Duke Town and our mission came first," said Mary.

"They do."

Suddenly a hollow in the embankment yawned on the right. Huts similar to those at Old Town sprawled along the riverbank. Now Mary could see they were mud huts roofed with what appeared to be palm leaves. Jutting up among them was a large and very ugly building covered with corrugated steel plates.

"The king's Iron Palace," commented Thomson dryly.

High above them on the right were white buildings, obviously of European making. Thomson pointed out the mission's buildings on one prominence he called "Mission Hill" and Britain's consular buildings on another rise.

"September 11, 1876," said Mary, too melodramatically. Self-consciously she returned her attention to the river and its shore. "Such a conglomeration."

The *Ethiopia* now entered a swarm of ships and boats that abutted the village. Between the river congestion and the many huts ashore were warehouses and loading docks. Nearest the shore on the river were dozens of canoes, each with a small thatched roof over its central area. One canoe was much larger and longer, with a shiny brass cannon mounted on the bow. Mary knew it must be the king's canoe. Farther out in the river were many of what appeared to be seaworthy European vessels, but all sails had been lowered from the masts, and the decks were shaded with mat roofing.

"Those are the ships of the palm-oil traders," said Thomson, "whom we land-lovers generally call 'ruffians,' for good reason." He shook his head. "They are more tightly controlled now by the British authorities than in the past. But they're still a tough lot, all more or less answering to a syndicate in Liverpool. They have nothing to do while they are here but wait for the Efiks to negotiate the trade with those natives who produce the palm oil. On board their ships the ruffians have their trade goods: raw brass and copper, food, firearms, gunpowder, cutlery, and plateware, as well as baubles like mirrors and beads."

"And what else?" probed Mary sternly.

"Yes, and sadly, also rum and gin. In any event, after the Efiks negotiate the trade, the ruffian will leave with a shipload of palm oil and the raw kernels. Most of the bloodshed between Europeans and natives has not been due to skullduggery in the trading itself but due to attempts to circumvent this system. Whites have tried to eliminate the middlemen, the Efiks. The Efiks have tried to eliminate the Liverpool palm-oil syndicate by hiring their own shipping. The result is always bloodshed."

Thomson's face brightened. "I say, here comes your welcoming committee!"

Floating toward the *Ethiopia* was a white boat rowed by four black men in immaculate white suits. Sitting under an awning on the boat were a bearded man in a dark suit and a woman in a gray dress. Mary recognized the missionary couple from their visits to Dundee. They were old enough to be her parents. She was sorry to see that in spite of their proper attire they looked very haggard.

"Reverend Anderson!" Mary shouted from the deck.

" 'Daddy' Anderson," he corrected. He turned to one of the natives in a white suit and said something. Then he turned again to Mary and explained, "The boatman is coming aboard to get your luggage. The boxes of supplies for the mission will have to be picked up tomorrow. They're in the hold."

Mary said good-bye to the Thomsons, who awaited another welcoming committee. Soon she and her luggage were being rowed ashore. The reverend's wife, she was told, was to be called "Mammy" Anderson. The nicknames *Daddy* and *Mammy* seemed very odd to Mary, but she could scarcely think anyway because she was so overwhelmed by new sights, new sounds, and especially new smells. Palm oil and rotting vegetation were not so unpleasant as they were overpowering in their richness. After Mary and the Andersons left the boat to trudge up the hill, gentle breezes dissipated the unctuous odors. Soon they walked on paths bordered by hedges of vivid red hibiscus. It was the entry into the mission compound. The Andersons pointed out the schoolhouse, the church, workshops, dormitories, and their own living quarters. Mary looked far down at the Calabar River and the sprawl of huts called Duke Town.

"So this is life in the jungle!" she remarked, immediately regretting how flippant it sounded. The Andersons looked so tired and worn out.

Daddy Anderson pointed out Government Hill in the distance. He described the ornate Residency, a Victorian house imported piece by piece from London. Inside it was elegant brass and mahogany, highlighted by a great hanging fan called a "punkah." A boy was stationed there to keep the fan stirring the air inside at all times.

"They have lovely English gardens there," he added, "Can you see the pretty red and yellow flowers on the grounds?"

"No, sir," she admitted.

"Of course she can't," agreed Mammy Anderson. "Come with me, lassie. I'll show you your room."

Mary's room was inside the main living quarters for the missionaries. The rooms were neither ornate nor large. But no girl raised in a one-room tenement apartment would think the room too small. An iron-framed cot was draped in mosquito netting. The feet of the cot stood in small cans of kerosene. So did the feet of a cupboard and a table.

"Ants," explained Mammy Anderson, noticing Mary's nose wrinkle at the smell of kerosene.

"It's cool in here," said Mary pleasantly.

"Africa is not hot like people believe," answered Mammy Anderson impatiently, "but the rain does keep it very wet." The old missionary was all business. "As you already know you'll teach in the school every day. And you'll be the first to rise in the morning because I want you to ring the wake-up bell at five-thirty. We have prayer every morning at six o'clock and every evening at six o'clock. You will also be at the Efik service at four o'clock. If you have any spare time you can visit the native houses down in Duke Town. If you ever want to visit one of the other towns like Old Town it's all right, just as long as you take some of the boatmen with you."

"Is it dangerous to go to the towns?"

"It's just a precaution," Mammy Anderson answered curtly.

"Leopards?" Mary blurted.

"It's always best to make a lot of noise in the jungle," commented Mammy Anderson. "Then you will never see a leopard."

Later, as they walked the grounds, Mary noted, "The sky is very blue and lovely. Yet you say it rains a lot?"

"The rain here is a bit peculiar." Mammy Anderson sighed as she studied the sky. "This is our third day like this. Calm and rather warm. It should have rained yesterday. Almost surely we will get rain this afternoon. Make sure you are close to shelter."

"Oh, a bit of rain won't hurt me. I'm not so sweet I'll melt."

"But you are so tiny you might blow away," Mammy Anderson shot back. "Be close to shelter," she repeated sternly. "Wait here a moment. I have to see the reverend. I believe he's here in the schoolhouse."

It seemed only moments later that the sky started to darken in the northeast. Lightning stabbed through the dark sky too. Thunder rolled over Calabar. Mary squinted hard in the direction of the storm. It almost seemed as if a dark wall were rushing toward her. Surely not. She had heard the sailors speak of such tempests at sea. Suddenly leaves and debris were swept off the grounds into the air. Wind struck her face in a fury.

"Get inside!" yelled Mammy Anderson.

She grabbed Mary's arm and bustled her inside the schoolhouse. Mary watched the storm at a window until Mammy Anderson slammed the shutters closed. Mary's ears were choked with the rage of winds assaulting the trees outside. Gusts pummeled the building. Thunder popped. Rain pelted the shelter now. She seemed drowning in noise. It was useless to try to speak. She stood transfixed, listening to the storm rage. Then ever so gradually the wind died down until she could hear soft rain. Mammy Anderson opened the window. Rain did fall gently now. Thunder still rolled but it was weak.

"The storm has sped by us to the southwest," said Mammy Anderson, then added very loudly, "Children, this is Miss Slessor."

Mary turned, shocked to realize she had been standing in a room full of children sitting at tables. They were all boys, perhaps six to ten years old. Had they calmly done their schoolwork in the storm? Or had they watched the redheaded newcomer as she was frozen in terror? Their black faces grinned at her. Yes, they enjoyed very much her first encounter with a Calabar storm.

"These wild storms come every few days for six months, May to October," said Mammy Anderson. "For some reason, they also let up a bit in August. One of the British officers said they are properly called 'line squalls.' We call them 'tornadoes.' Whatever you call them, don't let one of them catch you outside!"

So this was Africa.

FIVE

In the weeks that followed, Mary taught at the school, more often than not just holding up cards hour after hour to teach children the alphabet or simple arithmetic. One morning she overslept and rang the wake-up bell too late. Mammy Anderson withheld her supper that evening. But Daddy Anderson smuggled cookies and bananas to her. Mary learned that, although over a thousand Efiks attended Sunday services in all the missions in the Calabar area, the 30-year effort had harvested only 174 converts. This was no surprise to Mary at all. No one who had read the exploits of David Livingstone would be surprised at the difficulty of bringing Africans to Christ. Livingstone's mentor, the great Robert Moffat, converted only 40 Africans in his first 20 years at Kuruman. The thought of Livingstone tweaked Mary. After only a few weeks at Kuruman, Livingstone had plunged into the real frontier to live among the natives. Mary still had not ventured away from the flowered paths of Mission Hill!

"I don't care *where* I go as long as I go *forward*!" she reminded herself.

But who would accompany her beyond Mission Hill? The Efiks at the mission were always busy. Besides, teaching and performing all the other duties the Andersons had given her seemed to eat up her entire day. Still, she must find time.

One afternoon she put all excuses aside and forced herself to talk an Efik into walking down into Duke Town with her. Thus, she began descending from the breezy heights to visit the Africans sweltering down in Duke Town. The visits began awkwardly. At first she did little more than smile at the Efiks and show them she was willing. But she slowly picked up the language of the Efiks. She mainly visited converts in their fenced "yards." Standing beside their white-walled thatched huts she spoke to them about Christ. The exchange was always polite. There was no doubt that they were taken by Christ. Hope Waddell and his successors had truly converted some Efiks to Christ. Sometimes Mary was even able to help them with a problem.

But these true Christians aren't the only ones I must visit, she told herself. *Many come to services but are not converted. They present us with a real opportunity.*

So Mary memorized faces and sought them out in Duke Town. In the beginning her conversations with these candidates were always polite, too. A few actually were swayed by her. But most were sly, saying what they thought the missionary wanted to hear, with not an ounce of sincerity in their responses. These people, she decided, were attending services because they thought it was the shrewd thing to do. It opened doors for business.

Still, not all their conversation was insincere. And Mary learned much from them in their attempts to switch the subject away from Christianity. Did she know Calabar never got a real dry season like Lagos to the west? That was why it was hard to store vegetables here. That was why only the palm oil tree and cocoyams really grew well here. Back in the jungle it was very difficult to grow yams and corn because they needed lots of sun. Did she know that? Of course, manioc could be grown successfully back in the jungle just as long as it was cultivated under trees to protect it from too much rainfall. Did she know that? But these subjects were not inexhaustible. Repeated visits from Mary were met by many with growing sullenness, then surliness.

And what about those Efiks who do not come to services? she asked herself.

So in the yards of Duke Town she also visited this third group of Efiks. These people seemed neither sullen nor surly. They were just ignorant of Christ. She soon confirmed her suspicion that their pagan beliefs were not simple but quite complex. It was with this group of people she learned Efik fastest, gesturing energetically, aching to get just the right words of their language to tell them of the salvation offered by Christ. Soon she began to question why she confined her ventures to only their yards.

"Many of the Efiks put in very long workdays," she realized. "They cannot be found in their yards."

So Mary sought out Efik men at the docks. She met them coming back from their shrimping. She found Efik women pounding out their wash at the river. She discovered some women on the outskirts of Duke Town, ripping the husks off palm fruit, boiling the husks for the palm oil, and setting aside the kernels. Her ability to understand and speak Efik improved every day. Yet she still had a haunting doubt that she was not even meeting the real Efiks.

One day one of the boatmen approached her. The boatmen understood her limited Efik and knew some English themselves. "You do not feel good today?" the boatman asked in English.

"Why do you ask?"

"*Harmattan,*" he said simply.

Mary followed his eyes to the sky. Yes, the sky was peculiar. Calm and cloudless but strangely unlike the sky that foreshadowed the violent tornadoes. This sky today was not azure blue but a hazy blue, tinged pink. But how could that be?

"*Harmattan,*" repeated the boatman. "Dust from the north."

Yes, now she remembered. In the months of less rainfall—after all, Calabar never got a dry season—winds from vast deserts far to the north supposedly brought dust with them. So this was *harmattan*. She peered east where she could see the Cameroon Mountains anytime she bothered to look. Not today.

"Boatmen take you to Creek Town Sunday?" he offered helpfully.

Creek Town? The village of King Eyo Honesty VII? For Sunday services? She had not thought of that. There was so much work to do on Mission Hill and in Duke Town. But why shouldn't she go once?

So she asked Daddy Anderson, who shrugged a

very weary, "Why not?"

Mammy Anderson blinked as if to say, *What will this fireball of a lass do next?*

So the boatmen rowed Mary upstream to Creek Town Sunday morning. On the way the boatmen expounded on the Efik way of life. The king reigned over many subchiefs and their families. It was his clan or "house." Families were made up of freemen and slaves. Very often it was hard to tell a slave from a freeman. The only times it was bad to be a slave was when a king died or when the Egbo runners—the "vigilantes"—were loose.

"Then it is very bad to be a slave," one of the boatmen admitted.

Finally they arrived at Creek Town. Although Duke Town had its own King Archibong III, he was dominated by the mission and the British Consul. This was the first time Mary had seen a king in his full authority. King Eyo Honesty attended the church service, dressed in an elegant silk waistcoat and trousers—but no shirt or shoes. To Mary's amazement, after the service she was invited to lunch with the king as an honored guest. But first she toured Creek Town, guided by a subchief, until a cannon fired at two o'clock. Then with the subchief she entered the king's large hall. Sitting at the head of a long table was King Eyo Honesty, now wearing a shiny English top hat adorned with what appeared to be parrot feathers.

"Sit to the king's right," the subchief told her in Efik.

So Mary sat to his immediate right. Slowly the chairs filled on Mary's side of the table with the king's other white guests. To his left sat his black guests. Out of nowhere, it seemed, a woman offered Mary a basin. The woman was undressed from the waist up but this no longer startled Mary. It was native custom she saw as very innocent. The king watched Mary out of the corner of his eye. Mary saw the woman also carried a pitcher, so she extended her hands over the basin. She had guessed correctly. The woman poured water over her hands and another attentive woman patted her hands dry with a towel. The women continued on down the table to offer all guests this opportunity to wash their hands. Then several women entered the hall, balancing on their heads large silver platters and bowls covered with cloths. After all the platters and bowls were set on the table, the king clapped his hands. The cloths were ceremoniously removed.

"Lord, give me strength," prayed Mary as she studied the platters and bowls. She must eat anything that was offered. Perhaps she could take the initiative. "Oh, yams," she said enthusiastically in Efik, "stuffed with peppers!"

"Perhaps you would also like this," suggested the king in Efik.

Mary stared at a soup that looked like tar. What was in it? She couldn't tell. She ladled some of the soup into a bowl. She pretended the thick black soup was split-pea soup.

"Excellent," she exclaimed in Efik.

But she soon discovered she was expected to take a portion of everything. Another soup was served, this one a slurry of manioc and fish heads.

"Superb," she gushed, avoiding the staring fish eyes.

Then came mashed manioc, known as *fufu*. Then roast goat. Cocoyams. Corn. On and on. Much of the food was either fried in palm oil or submersed in palm oil. At first the king was aloof, but as Mary maintained her enthusiasm for the food, all while speaking more and more Efik, his attitude changed.

"You know our language well," he said in Efik.

"My mother back in Scotland has talked about Calabar ever since I was a little girl," she told him in labored Efik. "And the name of King Eyo Honesty is well known to us there."

"Is that so?" he said, trying to hide his pleasure at her flattery. "Perhaps I could write a letter to your mother," he suggested slyly.

King Eyo Honesty told a subchief that very moment to remind him to correspond with Mary's mother! Mary was startled, but not worried. She had told the truth. Her mother would be thrilled, and her mother's true interest in the king would shine through her words.

Mary left the king, feeling triumphant. But King Eyo Honesty was so Anglicized. Was she going to use this new friendship to avoid that which nagged at her conscience, entering the jungle to visit the real Efiks?

Tornadoes. Crocodiles. These I've seen with my own eyes, she warned herself. *Yet I know other dangers just as real lurk there too. Leopards. Snakes. Jungle fever.*

Did she dare go into the jungle? Boatmen accompanying her or not, the jungle was infested with a thousand things that made her skin crawl with dread. Yet she had to force herself to venture forth. Didn't she?

Fear of the jungle, Mary taunted herself in her room on sleepless nights. Such a childish solution, she finally realized. Courage comes from God. She delved into His Word. A Psalm soothed her: "Be of good courage, and he shall strengthen your heart, all ye that hope in the Lord." She gathered more comfort from Ezekiel: "though briers and thorns be with thee, and thou dost dwell among scorpions: be not afraid." Bolstered by other verses, she allowed herself to remember her exemplar.

What would Livingstone think of a missionary who clung to civilization like a baby to a blanket? She knew only too well. He had been disgusted with the missionaries who hung around Cape Town, afraid to venture forth. The "verandah" crowd, they were called contemptuously by adventurous people more indiscreet than Livingstone. She must resolve to venture away from Mission Hill, beyond Duke Town, beyond the king's well-spread table at the palace in Creek Town. She prayed for God to give her courage.

One morning she awoke full of courage. *This very day I shall find the boatmen!* she promised herself.

Mary felt vaguely sick though as she sought out the boatmen. In Duke Town she found them down at the docks, lounging in the missionary boat. They set to tidying the boat when they saw her approach. They didn't seem pleased when she asked them to take her to Old Town. And going there on foot definitely upset them. Mary hadn't thought of this reluctance at all. They had to stay with the boat, they insisted. She informed them only one of them had to stay with the boat. Grumbling, they drew straws to see who went and who stayed. The winner yelped his approval. He was the one who got to stay with the boat.

"Oh, come on," she said brightly to the other three.

"The walk will do you good. See if you can keep up with me!"

The boatmen began to respond to her good humor. That seemed to lift up her own spirits. Soon they were walking briskly on a path along the Calabar River.

Mary remembered to make a lot of noise. It was very easy for her. She felt freer than she had since she stepped off the *Ethiopia*. She watched the path carefully for snakes but that fear soon gave way. Wouldn't eight thumping feet scare snakes from the path?

In fact, Mary's fear of the jungle soon vanished. There was undergrowth but it was not impenetrable even away from the path. The tree trunks, smooth and as thick as three feet, burgeoned out into massive anchors at their bases. The trunks towered, almost branchless to a height of perhaps fifty or sixty feet, where they exploded into a large crown of glossy green leaves. The crowns of the trees coalesced into a leafy canopy for the forest. So the jungle was dark as dusk and yet it no longer scared Mary.

To make conversation Mary asked the names of trees and was surprised at how many different kinds there were, because the trees all looked very much alike to her. After they had walked awhile, it occurred to her that if one climbed a tree to a height of about twenty feet one could probably see far into the distance, right over the undergrowth and right below the canopy.

"Stop!" she said in Efik. She shed her shoes. "What is this tree?"

"Mahogany," said one of the boatmen in English.

The boatmen watched suspiciously, then dropped their jaws in disbelief. Mary was clambering up the trunk of the mahogany tree. Although the trunk appeared branchless there were enough small growths sticking out like rungs for her to easily rise twenty feet above the forest floor.

Yes, she had been right. One could see into the distance. Not far up the river were the drab huts of Old Town. Perhaps only half a mile. Did the boatmen know that? She slowly descended to the forest floor. It was much harder to climb down than climb up. She carefully put her shoes back on, not so fearless of the jungle she didn't shake them out first.

"Last one to Old Town is a monkey!" she yelled in Efik and dashed down the path.

She heard the boatmen behind her, breathless from running and laughing. One by one they careened past her. The race worked out just as she imagined. The boatmen stormed past the first huts, screaming and laughing in their white suits. Mary strolled into the village, hands folded, the quiet demure missionary lass to be sure. The boatmen laughed even harder as they realized what she had done.

"There is a Fattening House," said one of her companions when he stopped laughing.

How did the boatman know? Was it the unusually high matted fence that surrounded the hut? The hut, though large, appeared to be nothing unusual. Mary would have walked right past the enclosed yard if she had not been curious. The Efiks had a peculiar custom of fattening brides. The fatter the bride became, the more esteem it gave her family. After all, only the most prosperous family could afford to keep a daughter in total gluttony for perhaps as long as a year. Mary heard the girls were fed foods rich in fat and oil. The prospective brides stuffed themselves with nuts and starchy vegetables fried in palm oil. Finally a woman came out of the hut. On her head she wore a turban of bright blue silk. Her dress, also silk, was patterned with blue, red, and yellow flowers. She was not fat. She was startled by the sight of Mary.

"Efiks here never see a White Ma before," explained the boatman in English.

It was the first time they called Mary "Ma." It was strange to her ears, but she liked it. The boatmen said something in Efik to pacify the trembling woman, who appeared to manage the Fattening House. Still frightened, she snapped some words at the boatmen. They spoke back to her. Efik shot back and forth, impolite and too fast for Mary to understand. It sounded to Mary as if they asked to see one of the girls.

A boatman confirmed it, "She will get a fat girl for you to see, Ma."

Mary watched intently as the first woman led a young woman from the hut. The young woman barely got through the door. "Lord have mercy!" screamed Mary. The young woman was just as startled by Mary. She stopped eating something and gasped. The young woman seemed as wide as she was tall. She bobbed and jiggled like pudding. Her face was so fat her eyes were slits. Surely she weighed 250 pounds. With her was a slender girl—a slave, Mary guessed—who turned her back on Mary and kept prompting the fat young woman to eat from a plate of what appeared to be some kind of gooey candy.

With much effort Mary now talked to the woman

who ran the Fattening House. The woman must have been offended by Mary's tone because she explained defensively that there was much more to a Fattening House than fattening. The girl was taught etiquette. The girl was taught the duties of marriage. The girl's purity was rigorously protected while in the Fattening House.

Mary thanked the women and walked away slightly dazed. Soon she turned to the boatmen. "Do you really desire a girl that fat?"

"The great fatness is to honor the father, not the groom," one of them answered sourly.

He went on to explain what he considered Efik beauty in a woman. Yes, plump was desirable. But every Efik man knew no wife could maintain her Fattening House weight and do any real work. The girl should at least keep her arms and hips plump but she should display a waist too. She should have all her teeth, strong and white. Her hair should be long, never short, but neatly braided. The boatman grew dreamy-eyed as he described feminine perfection.

"Thank you," said Mary, breaking his trance.

A few moments later they surprised a small girl jabbing a stick into an ant pile. The girl glanced up, saw Mary, and screamed. Before Mary could calm her fears the child dashed into the jungle. The boatmen laughed. So did several women in the yard of a hut nearby.

Why weren't they frightened? They were braiding each other's hair. But their movements were slow and wobbly. Mary felt sick. She knew too well that glazed look in their eyes, that satisfied but stupid expression on their faces. The women were half drunk. How could that be? She saw green gin bottles on the ground. The boatmen rebuked the women for her. The women seemed to realize for the first time that Mary had a white face. They seemed to know she was behind the boatmen's righteousness. They scowled at Mary.

"What business is our drinking to her?" they clamored. "We worked hard to collect the palm kernels, and now we are enjoying our pay!"

Mary snapped in Efik, "I see now the Efik women must be cleansed first, or the men will never change either!"

Some men did lounge around the next hut, even drunker than the women. They had both rum and gin.

Mary put her hands on her hips. "Shame on you men," she fumed. "In broad daylight, too."

The three boatmen began bantering with the men. The men made it known they had heard of White Mas. But they didn't know a White Ma had hair the color of flames!

One of them piped up proudly that he had even been to Duke Town once. What was this White Ma doing here anyway? Causing trouble?

The drunken men ranted on and on. Mary rebuked them. How could they provide for their families? How could they defend their families? How could they discipline their families? There was much anger at her own father in her reproaches. Finally Mary pushed on.

One of the boatmen said not so innocently, "Some men ask why White Mas and White Pas trade rum and gin to Efiks for palm oil if it's so bad for Efiks?"

Mary couldn't answer him.

SIX

Yes, the boatman's question was a stinging rebuke. Had these men and women been drunk on their own palm wine or some kind of native beer before the traders came? Or had the high-powered distilled liquor of the white world done this to them? How could she know for sure?

Further on, by a small hut, sat a man looking very miserable.

Mary stopped. "What is the matter?" she asked.

"My little boy has died," he answered, so much in grief he had no fear of her.

The boatman explained to Mary the man was sitting by a devil hut where the boy was buried. Food was stored in the hut for the boy's spirit to eat. But the family mourned and fasted. Painstakingly Mary herself explained with gestures and Efik to the man that the Almighty God had his son.

"God took the boy?" the man asked. "He wasn't

killed by the witchcraft of an enemy?"

"No," answered Mary.

Mary left, sensing the man was about to give up his pagan mourning. But she knew by now that all Efiks thought death before extreme old age was the result of witchcraft.

That was part of the reason why it was such a calamity when a "king" died. No better—or worse—example could be found than the death of King Eyamba, the baron who had inhabited the garish Iron Palace in Duke Town. He had died in 1847, right before the eyes of the pioneer missionary Hope Waddell.

The dead king's subchiefs dug a great hole in the floor of the palace and placed the dead king there on a sofa. Then the "king began to call his loved ones." The subchiefs ordered each of his dozens of wives to dress in their finest silk and to drink a large mug of rum. Then the subchiefs strangled the stupefied wives one by one with a silk handkerchief. The dead wives were stacked neatly beside the king.

After that the subchiefs murdered all the king's slaves and stacked them near the king.

Then the trials with the poisonous esere bean were held. After all, according to Efik belief, someone had to be responsible for the witchcraft that killed the king. So the subchiefs brought in all those considered unfriendly to the king. Each was required to drink the potion made from the esere bean. Once in a great while the accused would vomit the poison quickly enough to survive, but that was very rare. And if a subchief had his own quarrel with the one on trial, he would rush in to hack the accused to death before the bean worked its "justice" anyway.

Soon the grave in the Iron Palace contained hundreds of stacked corpses. The subchiefs stopped at last. Surely they had satisfied the king's honor according to their sacred custom.

The missionaries bitterly protested against human sacrifice to the Efik kings. They demanded the custom stop.

The next test came in 1855 when King Willy Tom Robins died in Old Town itself. Many were murdered to join him in his grave. Although the missionaries railed against the heinous practice, they were outraged when the British Consul ordered the *H. M. S. Antelope* to bombard Old Town as a warning to all Efiks. Volley after volley from the ship's cannons burned Old Town to the ground.

The next test came in 1858 when the king of Duke Town died. Not one wife or slave was known to be sacrificed, Mary had been told.

Praise God, that custom has been stopped, she applauded to herself. But on more reflection she wondered with a shudder, *Or has it?* Because talk among the missionaries was that humans were still sacrificed around the fringes of Duke Town and Creek Town—but on a much smaller scale and secretly. Moreover, back among the Efiks and other tribes in the hinterlands who could doubt such things did not still occur on a large scale?

"And just who is doing anything about it?" she asked herself in English, startling the boatmen as the four of them trudged back to Duke Town. Then she startled them even more by answering herself, "No one!"

During the day with all her many duties Mary could forget about the Efiks and other tribes in the hinterlands and the terrible things that happened to them—but not at night. Silence led to prayer, and prayer led to love and truth.

And just who is doing anything about it? she continued to ask herself.

She could imagine her hero Livingstone in such circumstances. She hadn't the slightest doubt he would have resolved immediately to find such people and change them. But Livingstone was a man. A great one at that. How could she, a tiny woman, do it? But that was a lame excuse; history was full of courageous women.

Now every night the need to forge into the hinterlands gnawed at her, as once the need to plunge into the jungle had. Mary now realized she loved the Efik people away from Duke Town and Creek Town. Yes, they had severe problems with liquor and violent customs, but they were still Efiks. Many of the Efiks in Duke Town were corrupted, no longer Efik but not Christian either. Sly, they said what they thought the missionary wanted to hear, with not an ounce of sincerity. Their innocence seemed lost.

"Lord, have mercy on them. They have fallen in love with rum and gin and iron pots and shiny English plates!"

Mary continued her brief sorties into the jungle. Her Efik improved. She understood the fast-talking jungle people more and more. But her time for self-education was limited. Moreover, her energy lessened. How well she now understood that weary look she had seen on the missionaries in her first days in Calabar.

The dry, dust-bearing winds of the *harmattan* scoured the strength right out of Mary. She came to dread them. The first *harmattan* season in late 1876 made her feel tired and nauseated much of the time. The second in 1877 affected her more, but the third one in 1878 sapped her energy the way it did many of the natives. She was not just bone-tired and slightly sick at her stomach every day, but her eyes hurt. Her nose bled. Her throat felt like dry sandpaper. Her lips were chapped. Her fingernails cracked. How she came to hate the *harmattan*. And its effects on her were growing worse each year. Finally she was leveled by alternating chills and fevers.

By spring she knew the truth. "It was not the *harmattan* that leveled me after all."

Nor was it the very prevalent elephantiasis, a grotesque swelling of the limbs caused by some kind of worm. Nor was it blood flukes. Nor *loa loa*, the loathsome eye worm so common around Calabar. Nor the dreaded leprosy, known from the Bible and common in the palm-oil region. Nor did she suffer from the nasty Guinea worms that caused blisters and boils. Nor yellow fever. Nor river blindness. Nor sleeping sickness carried by the tsetse flies. Nor hookworm from her bare-footed adventures. . .

"Jungle fever," pronounced Daddy Anderson with his experience of many years.

"Yes, it is most certainly jungle fever," agreed the doctor who had been summoned from the residency on Government Hill to see Mary.

"I won't 'give in' to jungle fever," croaked Mary from her bed.

She remembered well Livingstone's advice about jungle fever in *Missionary Travels*. The fever affected the mind.

Most victims became very depressed and irritable. The funniest joke could not bring a glimmer of a smile. Often these feelings of gloom appeared even before the fever. But at any rate Mary knew she had to fight these feelings. She remembered Livingstone's own special remedy for fever, won by his dozens of bouts with the disease.

"Mix resin of jalap and calomel, eight grains each," she told Daddy Anderson groggily, "with four grains each of rhubarba and quinine. . . ."

"Now, Mary, let the doctor do it."

She knew now that she had suffered from jungle fever for weeks and not known it. She had chills, then a deadening fever. Over and over. She had forced herself to work right through them. Not this last time though. Her chills had been the worst ever. She now began the battle with the fever that followed. This fever already made every part of her ache. Even her hair hurt. The doctor began giving her periodic doses of medicine, which she knew surely contained quinine. But as wonderful as quinine was, it was a poison. It ravaged the body in order to kill whatever caused the fever. At one point she awoke from the fever to discover she was deaf. If she had not read Livingstone, she would have been terrified. She would have been sure she was dying. *Isn't the sense of hearing the last faculty a dying person loses?* But she knew that with quinine treatment deafness or ringing in the ears was a sign the fever was about broken!

Finally one morning she awoke, and for once the bedding was not soaked. "What day is it?" she asked Mammy Anderson who was sitting nearby.

"It's in the month of June, Mary."

"June! I must get back to work."

"You'll do nothing of the sort! There's a steamer leaving for Liverpool next week, and you'll be on it for a furlough. Don't think it's great favor to you either, lassie. You must talk up the mission when you're back there."

So in June of 1879 Mary sailed for Britain. She read her Bible aboard the steamer and fretted over talking in public about the mission. She would rather face a leopard on a shaded jungle path than face a crowd of judgmental Scots. In fact, she had once encountered a leopard, a young one, no doubt, because the older ones were never seen. To the boatmen's gap-jawed astonishment she had sung to the leopard. Verses from Psalm 50 seemed appropriate at the time, especially "For every beast of the forest is mine, and the cattle upon a thousand hills." The leopard blinked at her serenade and slipped back into the brush. Yes, she would most definitely prefer soothing that beast to speaking to a crowd. Especially men. The thought of addressing men made her ill just to think about it. It was irrational, she knew. But the fear was all too real.

"Land ahoy!" yelled a sailor after many days in the open sea and one day in the Irish Sea.

Mysteriously, the men on the mission board had insisted that from Liverpool she return to Dundee on the train. Near the end of her journey, as she approached the Firth of Tay, whose bright waters shimmered on the south shore of Dundee, she understood why. A colossal rail bridge had been constructed two miles across the Tay. She was told by a trainman the bridge had been finished only the year before. As she approached from the south it almost seemed she saw Dundee for the first time. From the Tay the factory city sprawled up a slope to Dundee Law, a volcano so ancient it was ground down to a large hill.

It was a wonderful surprise, although she expressed her concern to the trainman about the stability of the bridge.

"You needn't worry your pretty little head about this bridge, lassie," he replied.

Once home in Dundee she drove the fear of speaking in public out of her mind by basking in the attention of her doting mother and two sisters. Mother seemed part of Calabar since she and the king had begun writing letters to each other. But Mary found she no longer had any tolerance for the life-draining tenements. Enough was enough. She had to get her mother and sisters out of the slums. In a flurry of activity she found a cottage in Downfield, a country village near Dundee. She assured them they could afford it because she would send them more of her salary. But in fact she would have to be assigned to another post in Calabar away from Mission Hill. For the truth was that she had to pay room and board out of her meager salary, and Mission Hill was by far the most expensive of the stations in Calabar. New missions were being opened though. Oban, Uyanga, and Ibami had just been added. There was even talk of opening a mission at Ikotana, far up the Cross River. Her own choice was an area in the hinterlands between the two far outposts of Ikorofiong and Iknetu but east of the Cross River. It was inhabited by the Okoyong tribe. The area itself was called "the Okoyong." She would ask to start a new mission there.

"But my obligation to speak for the missions can no longer be delayed," she admitted to her family, once they were settled in Downfield.

When she was called to speak to a group of ladies in a small hall, her old fear returned. Remembering Livingstone did not bolster her either because he had suffered from the same fear. He too dreaded "spouting off" in public, as he called it. Her heart beat like the executioner's ax as the moment to begin speaking approached. "God, grant me strength," she prayed.

Mary faced her audience. "Ladies. . ."

As she surveyed the listeners her voice froze in her throat. A man had entered near the back and quietly sat down. Mary was overcome. What a malady! It was so embarrassing. Yet she could not speak. She felt as if she were suffocating. It was all she could do to whisper to the chairwoman that the man must leave. The chairwoman looked at her in disbelief, then very reluctantly went to the back of the hall and asked the man to leave. Everyone looked puzzled. Was Mary going to speak of things only a woman could hear? But no, she did not, they soon discovered.

"My dear," said the chairwoman later, "what was the matter?"

"If only I knew," agonized Mary.

What was it about men? Oh yes, she knew it probably had something to do with her father. But what made her feel so self-conscious? So inadequate? The same kind of thing happened again the next time she began speaking. This time Mary had someone ask the man to sit where he could not watch her, and perhaps she would be able to continue. And she was able to speak, somehow secure in the knowledge that he was not watching her. It was a very embarrassing phobia she had. After awhile she and the ladies who knew her accepted it as a "thorn" in her side.

"Whatever the 'thorn' was that Saint Paul endured," she told her mother, "I, too, endure a humiliation as I speak for the mission."

"Perhaps it is a reminder not to get too bigheaded," said her mother.

But Mary's problem seemed small just before New Year's Eve of 1879. A fierce storm tore at Dundee. Even that did not rock the Slessors like the news about the great rail bridge across the Firth of Tay. It had collapsed in the storm. Worst of all, it carried a train into the Tay. At least seventy-five passengers and crew were plunged into a briny grave. Mary prayed for the unfortunates and had to wonder if the proud trainman had been one of those who perished.

Bearing her affliction, Mary spoke more and more of the crying need for missionaries in the hinterlands. How many poor Efiks and other tribes died needlessly because of their barbaric human sacrifices? Moreover, it wasn't only when kings died that these terrible things happened. She had heard many "houses"—not in Duke Town or Creek Town but in other villages—offered a sacrifice once a year to the river or to the jungle or to the sky. One ritual was to stake a man down in low tide as a sacrifice to the god of shrimps. After the next high tide the man was gone. She had heard from reliable people that Egbo runners often hanged their victims or impaled them—even on the outskirts of Duke Town! There were special places for these sacrifices, places whose sight sent shivers through every Efik slave.

"Some practices among the tribes in the hinterlands

are so barbaric I can not bring myself to speak of them," she told the ladies of the church.

She hoped and prayed the stories of murdering twins at birth were just horror stories the Efiks liked to tell. But she knew many of the other horrifying stories were true. So she told them to the ladies to enlist their sympathy. The men of the church were not denied her same tales of Calabar that the ladies heard. In small informal gatherings Mary could speak to men. Of course in the church circles of Dundee she often saw her old friend James Logie, now an influential member of the Foreign Mission Board. She told him of her burning desire to get away from Mission Hill and evangelize among the real Efiks, or even among the Okoyong. And she had to admit to him privately that she now had another reason. It would be cheaper to live at an outpost. The money she would save was needed by her mother and two sisters.

"There's talk of placing all missionary women in an auxiliary, giving you ladies more independence, more flexibility, more voice," he told her.

"Wonderful," she said.

"But it may not be proposed to the board until next year. Then, the implementation might take awhile. . . ."

Why was he telling her? Would it bear on her present circumstance? Or was he apologizing because it would *not* bear on her present circumstance? At any rate, she remembered to thank the Lord that women missionaries might be more independent—someday.

"You will be sailing back to Calabar with Reverend Goldie and his wife," James Logie told her in the fall of 1880.

"What a privilege," she gushed.

Yet she struggled against disappointment. For she was leaving Scotland with no word from the Foreign Mission Board about her request to be reassigned to any mission but Mission Hill above Duke Town. Nor was there any word about the new auxiliary that might have entertained her request. Still, she must trust God. She resolved to make thorough use of the voyage reading the Bible and having godly conversations with the Goldies. Reverend Goldie was one of the pioneer missionaries of Calabar. He was so accomplished a linguist he was revising Hope Waddell's vocabulary book on the Efik language. Often on the voyage Mary spoke Efik with him. Once in a while the reverend found himself deferring to Mary's understanding of what an Efik word meant. He seemed astonished that she could have picked up so much Efik in just three years. But he seemed to be judging her, weighing her, during their conversations. What did it mean?

It was October of 1880 when their ship steamed up the great estuary of the Cross River. Mary joked, "And we've just returned to several months of the weather I dislike most—the *harmattan*."

Reverend Goldie laughed. "Perhaps the *harmattan* is not so bad in Old Town."

"Old Town?" she gasped.

"Yes, my dear young lady, that is where you are assigned."

Old Town! She was astonished. So that was why Reverend Goldie studied her so intently. Surely he had been given the task of evaluating her capabilities during the month-long voyage. She was even more amazed to learn no other white missionary would go with her to Old Town. She was staggered. It seemed only yesterday she was the inexperienced newcomer—a brat even—who overslept and had to be sent to bed without supper. Many of her experiences had been related by other missionaries as wild, irresponsible escapades of youth: the foot races, the tree climbing, the singing to a leopard. Now this. Praise God for this great opportunity. Praise God that Reverend Goldie saw competence in her. Praise God for the Andersons, who must have seen competence in her too. Because, after all, they would never trust a mission to someone who was a wild irresponsible youth. She seemed to grow in her own eyes.

Yes, I will most definitely succeed in Old Town, she vowed. *With the Lord's help, of course.*

SEVEN

Mary's arrival in Old Town was greeted by a human skull leering at her from the top of a pole!

"Be gone, you devil," she barked.

The boatmen carrying her belongings were not surprised at all by talk of the devil. Or witches. Or any kind of witchcraft. It was the way in these remote villages. In spite of the macabre warning, Mary was remembered in Old Town. People gathered around her as she strolled through the village. She had visited these Efiks many times since the first time with the boatmen. She had spoken their language. She had raced their children. She had given them medicine and climbed their trees.

The chief appeared.

"I have come to live in the house of the missionaries," she said.

"Come with me, White Ma," he answered. "Where have you been? We thought you were dead."

The chief took Mary to the abandoned hut that

had served earlier failed missionary efforts. It was much like all the huts of the village. The walls were not mud brick but a framework of poles interwoven with smaller branches, then plastered with mud. The roof was mats of palm leaves. Its only luxury was an interior that had been whitewashed. All articles inside had been gutted long ago. Mary knew the hut could not be as old as it looked. After all, the British had burned Old Town to the ground in 1855. So perhaps this hut was only fifteen or twenty years old.

She laughed to herself. "Yes, I believe I can afford the rent here in Old Town."

With palm leaves she and the boatmen swept the cobwebs from the ceiling and walls, sending more than a few insects, spiders, and lizards scurrying. She and the boatmen removed all the debris from the floor of the hut. Then they washed walls and floors with water from the river. Finally the boatmen carried inside a tiny dresser and set up Mary's iron cot. They stood back, impressed with their efforts. *Home sweet home*, their eyes seemed to say. Then the boatmen departed.

"I need a woman to help me," Mary told the chief. "I will pay her."

Soon Mary had several young women asking about the job. They were very frightened, obviously there against their wills. She tried to put them at ease with her Efik, her directness, and her quiet manners. She asked questions of them to judge which of them might be the most compassionate with children. Because, after all, the education of the children was her main task. That education included knowing the Father, the Son, and the Holy Spirit. No one was educated who did not know Him. Her years of teaching at Mission Hill had made Mary skilled at winning confidence with children. But she was good with women too. She had decided on her very first trip to Old Town that the barbarism of the Efiks would never stop if the women were not changed before the men.

"Have any twins been born here lately?" she asked the woman she had chosen to be her helper.

"None to talk about," said the woman, frightened.

Mary didn't press the issue. The evasive answer told her what she suspected. With the help of the chiefs she set up a schedule. Her mission was not just Old Town. Requesting her help were the chiefs of three other villages, all between the Calabar River and the Kwa River, all even more remote than Old Town. The largest village was Kwa. The other two were Akim and Ikot Ansa. Soon Mary was so busy she had to hire helpers in these places, too. Most of the time she and her assistants taught young and any older Efiks who wanted to learn. And there were many older ones who did.

"Such a thirst for new ways!" marveled Mary. "I'll have them flocking to Christ."

She also administered simple medical treatment, especially for infections. And on the Lord's Day, although she could not minister the sacraments of baptism and holy communion, she conducted Sunday schools and church services. Boys rang bells to summon people to the services. Every Sunday morning she trekked to Kwa to minister to nearly a hundred Efiks; then she went on to Akim and Ikot Ansa on alternating Sundays to minister to half that many. After that she returned to Old Town to hold its services. The attendance there was highest of all. In the chief's yard she set up a table covered with a white cloth. There she displayed the Bible and the cross. As evening set in she lit the table with a lamp. By the time all services were concluded, she and her helpers walked back to the hut by lamplight.

"I'll not be such a dolt any longer as to dress for a London tea party," she said one day.

After that at her missions she still carried an umbrella and wore a full skirt. Her clothes were properly long-sleeved and buttoned at the neck. But no longer would she suffer petticoats. And after a while she no longer cinched in the dress at the waist. It billowed out like a tent. A "Mother Hubbard" the British sailors called such a dress. Many days Mary now cast aside her shoes. And no great hat would flop on her head—nor a small one. So she wore no hat at all and had her helper crop her long hair. The flaming tresses fell to the floor of the hut. The helper eagerly picked them up as Mary parted her short hair neatly on the left side. To Mary's astonishment later she discovered the helper sold her sunny hair.

In the next services Mary had to tell the Efiks sternly, "You can keep my hair as a momento if you're so foolish, but it must never be used as some kind of aid to bewitch or bless!"

Mary had discovered, as Livingstone had, that it was best to simply forge ahead with plans. Yes, be polite to the chiefs. But no, don't ask their permission. In their ignorance and uneasiness with something new they were almost certain to say no. If they were truly displeased with something she had done, they would tell her soon enough.

One of her first objectives was to give them a real sense of guilt about drinking alcohol. So she ranted against it, well supported by God's words in the Bible. After several months she had become a real "White Ma" to the Efiks. If she saw a woman drinking rum she would fly into her, then calmly tell the shaken woman why it was wrong to drink. There were more than enough reasons to convince any sensible person. As Mary had decided before, she concentrated on reforming the women first.

When the time came, could she treat men that same tough, demanding way? She wasn't sure. Her fear of speaking to men still gnawed at her. What would she do if an Efik man menaced her?

She did not wish that to happen. "But among people with violent customs such an incident seems certain sometime in my future," she concluded apprehensively.

One day Mary was southeast of Old Town, traipsing back from a remote village. They were passing a few huts scattered along the path. Drums suddenly pounded. The very jungle seemed to tremble, anxious and desperate. Her helper's eyes ballooned with fear.

"*Ifehe*, Ma!" screamed her helper. "Run!"

But Mary did not run. The helper dashed recklessly inside the hut of a complete stranger. Someone yelped angrily inside. Outside, everywhere Efiks were scrambling into huts. Women yanked their children roughly off the ground before disappearing. Some, too distant from the huts, plunged into the jungle. Only a few men still stood about, grinning.

"We are freemen," bragged one.

"So what?" asked Mary, puzzled.

"Egbo," explained another man vaguely, shrugging.

73

Was Mary at long last going to see an Egbo runner? Surely that was what this mad scramble meant. For some reason the Egbo runner was coming to punish someone. Perhaps any slave he found outside. Who knew?

"No!" screamed the high-pitched voice of a woman.

Suddenly a woman burst into view. Screaming, she ran along the path toward the huts. A figure was now close behind. Surely it was a wiry-muscled man, but he wore a large hideous mask, and his body was covered with vividly colored triangles. Worst of all he brandished a whip. A lash caught the woman across the back and seemed to paralyze her. She fell. Other men appeared, also wearing masks and painted garishly.

"Hold her," wheezed one of the Egbo runners breathlessly.

"We give her Egbo," growled another of the runners.

There were now four men around the woman. One wrestled with her, trying to subdue her kicking body. She was dirty and covered with leaves.

Mary could tolerate no more. Whether they were going to whip the woman or violate her some other way Mary did not know. Their intentions were violent and unjust. *God, arm me with courage,* she prayed.

"You stop that!" shouted Mary.

The men turned to gawk, even the one wrestling the woman. They seemed baffled by this strange white woman. Where had she come from? She wasn't dressed like the missionary women. She had hair the color of fire! Was she a white witch?

Mary marched right at them. "Let her go!" she snapped.

The nearest Egbo runner swung his whip at her. It

whirred past her face, missing. Another lashed at her. It missed too. Mary realized their misses were deliberate.

She had met the bluff of bullies before. She jabbed at the men with her umbrella, also deliberately missing. They began to dance around her, screaming and lunging at her.

Mary saw the woman slip away in the confusion. In seconds the poor woman had disappeared into the heavy brush. If Mary could keep these men occupied for a while longer they would never find the woman in the jungle. Mary snapped and snarled at the dancing Egbo runners, jabbing at them with her umbrella. When she was certain the woman had escaped, she struck the nearest runner with the umbrella.

"Ugh!" grunted the Egbo as he clutched his stomach.

She swatted another runner across the head with her umbrella. "Oweee!" he screamed.

They chattered to each rapidly in Efik. What was going on here? Who was this fiery-haired banshee? They either had to stop her or vanish. They could whip her good. She deserved it. Yes, they cheered each other, she surely deserved a thorough thrashing. Maybe a little salt rubbed in the wounds too! But would her injuries bring the British guns on their big ships? The elders had talked much of the Old Town that had been leveled by terrible guns. When one of the balls thumped into the earth it exploded, and it was as if a thousand guns were fired into the village. And what would the village chiefs do to these Egbo runners if they caused the British guns to come? Suddenly the Egbo runners sprinted down the jungle path and disappeared.

"Egbos, phooey!" spat Mary triumphantly.

It wasn't like her to flaunt a success, but she had to show the Efiks, especially her helper and the slaves, that Egbo runners must not be respected.

She wasn't about to forget that Egbo runners often meted out death. And she had heard of an insidious practice of "buying Egbo." In other words, if an Efik slave had money he might be able to pay them off. That showed Mary more than anything that many of the Egbos were nothing but thugs. What would happen to these bullying Egbo runners if they were met with force by slaves? The slaves had tried it once with their own secret society of Blood Men. But the real resistance must come from all slaves and as many sympathetic freemen as possible.

She couldn't help feeling she had been very lucky this time. But what was she thinking? It was not luck.

"It was Christ's strength," she admitted.

At times the backward customs of the Efiks seemed insurmountable to her. One of their practices went back centuries. Somehow the Efiks had arrived in the Calabar area and became middlemen between white traders and the native peoples back in the hinterlands. If anyone— white skinned or black skinned, it didn't matter—tried to circumvent their stranglehold on trade, he was murdered. Occasionally Mary would help an unusually adventurous man from the hinterlands take his produce to a white trader, but it was very dangerous business. She only became involved to prevent bloodshed.

"You must not try it again," she would warn the man, although it tore at her heart to discourage such boldness. "You must wait for the whites to come to you." Always nagging at Mary was that need to open up the hinterlands.

One of the most vile customs of the Efiks was toward twins. Mary had long hoped the stories of Efiks murdering twin babies were nothing but horror stories Efik men liked to tell. But she began to suspect more and more that such murders were going on. She heard unguarded comments by gossiping women. She saw the most peculiar sadness in the faces of some mothers who had just given birth. Had the poor mother disposed of one of the twin babies in order to save at least one of them?

Mary had asked more than one physician on her furlough back in Dundee. "Just how common is the birth of twins?" "About one in a hundred," they answered confidently.

Why would it be any different here in Africa? Yet, had she ever seen twin babies or twin children in all her visits to Duke Town or Creek Town or Old Town or the many little villages?

"No. Not one set of twins in thousands!"

She sought out an honest man. Perhaps in a subtle way she could draw out his opinion of twins without alarming him into silence. He was one who helped her often and seemed incapable of telling a lie. For that reason he was considered rather foolish.

"Kwano," she said one day, "have you seen the many twin children of the tribes far over to the west beyond the Cross River?"

"Twins!" he gasped in horror.

"What is wrong?"

"I don't know these faraway tribes, but a man cannot be the father of twins."

"Why not?"

"Everyone knows that a man can father only one child."

"But where does the other child come from?"

"That is just the problem, White Ma," he said earnestly. "The other child must be a devil-child."

"But how do you know which is which?"

"You don't."

"But what do you do?"

"Both babies are placed in a clay pot and carried far back into the forest," Kwano explained.

"Is that why I never see any twins?"

"Perhaps," he answered nervously.

More and more Mary began to suspect what Kwano said was true. And she began to suspect many of the Efik women got around the death sentence on twins by murdering one of them. If the pregnant woman's own mother and grandmothers were her midwives at birth, they could conspire to keep the birth of twins a secret. It wasn't that hard. Men never witnessed births. Mary also learned that if an Efik woman was discovered to be a mother of twins by the Efik men, she was either murdered or cast out into the jungle. After all, to have a devil-child she must have submitted to the desires of a devil! So the murder of one twin by the close-mouthed women in an Efik family seemed the lesser of two terrible evils.

One day in Old Town, Mary's helper said, "A trader comes to see you."

The appearance of a white man in Old Town was a rare event but not unknown now. White traders began to show up in Old Town now in the belief Mary had pacified the savages. In her yard Mary looked up from her work with the children. Never had she seen such an odd sight. The grimy, unshaven man cradled a bundle of rags in his arms.

"I found this orphan child upriver, Miss Slessor," he said.

Mary peeked inside the rags. "It's a baby girl, not more than a day or two old!"

"I can't do anything for her," said the trader. "Will you take her?"

Mary took the baby girl inside her hut. What choice did she have? She would somehow find what she needed for the child. The trader asked her to look at some trade goods in his boat. She left the baby in the care of her helper and walked the trader back to his boat on the Calabar River. All the way there he seemed to want to speak but kept his silence as he glanced around at the Efiks of Old Town. It was only at his boat, when the two of them were out of earshot of all Efiks, that he spoke.

"I found that baby girl upriver in a clay pot," he whispered. "Her twin brother was in the pot too."

"A twin! Was the poor boy dead?"

"No. I have him in the boat."

"I see. You didn't want to bring them together. I know a woman, a good friend, who will care for the boy until I can take him later. That way the Efiks will think he is just another orphan."

"We were lucky to find these twins alive," said the trader. "Very often they kill the babies before they put them in the pot."

"And the mother?"

"I know nothing of the mother. I'm sorry."

Holding the baby boy in her arms, Mary watched

the man row downriver toward Duke Town. He was rough but he had a good heart.

She walked numbly to the hut of Yaba, a Christian mother Mary knew would nurse the boy. So it was true that the Efiks still murdered twins. She must speak out against this outrage in the services. She must continue to speak against the Egbo runners too. They were still very active. She spoke against human sacrifice too. It was much subdued but a harsh reminder from her was not too cautious. And she spoke against slavery.

Of all their evil customs slavery was the hardest to raise any indignation against. "Did not the Jews of the Bible—God's chosen people—keep slaves?" asked one very precocious Efik. In fact, Mary had to admit that if human sacrifice and the Egbo runners were banned, there was little difference between slave and freeman. Moreover, the Efiks foolishly sent far more slaves to school than freemen!

"Meanwhile, I will take in any twin I can find—or any orphan for that matter," she vowed. "I'll christen my new children "Janie," after my little sister Jane, and "Robby," after my poor departed brother."

Home deputies from the Foreign Mission Board visited Mary in 1882. She had nothing to hide and much to show. Due to her harangues there was less public drunkenness in the villages in her charge than there was in other regions around Calabar. She now preached to hundreds on a regular basis. She and her helpers, numbering a dozen, taught hundreds of children. And not just children. Some of the grownup Efiks still attended school too, convinced this was too great an opportunity to miss.

Plus, Mary had a number of orphans she was raising. "You might well consider appointing some ladies to perform this child-rearing duty alone," she instructed the deputies. The deputies seemed very impressed except for her own adaptations to the jungle. They blinked perceptibly at her appearance: shorn hair, hatless, often barefooted, in a dress as shapeless as a tent. Had her rebellious appearance canceled out all the good she had accomplished?

"The deputies were very affected by you," Daddy Anderson told her at Mission Hill later. "Favorably," he added when he noticed her look of doubt. "They will most certainly give a glowing report of your accomplishments to the Foreign Mission Board. And your success will surely hasten the creation of an auxiliary."

"Praise God for that," she said. "And when do you suppose I'll get an assignment in the hinterlands?"

"Oh, lassie, I don't know about that," he groaned.

But when Mary returned to Old Town she had an invitation that seemed too good to be true.

EIGHT

This is my golden opportunity to be among the raw heathen!" she exclaimed after reading a letter.

Not up the Cross River but down the great estuary on its far west side was the village of Ibaka, a good thirty miles away from Old Town. It was virtually on the sea but very isolated. Its chief was Okon. Mary had met him once in Creek Town, where he was a guest of King Eyo Honesty. Okon had invited her to come to Ibaka. King Eyo Honesty was involved in the effort too, for there was also a letter from him offering her the use of his royal canoe. More than that, the canoe was to arrive at a certain date!

"How can I refuse?" she said with glee.

Her only regret was leaving behind some of her *bairns*, a Scottish word she used for her house children or orphans. She could take four of the older house children with her. But the youngest, especially the twins, would have to stay behind—Janie with Mary's assistant and

Robby with Mary's friend Yaba. Mary went about quietly preparing for the trip but soon realized the word was out: White Ma was leaving to visit a chief in the wilds!

"Be careful among the savages!" warned the Old Towners

"If they harm a hair on Ma's head we will avenge her," they vowed to each other.

"Vengeance is the Lord's," she told them.

But some of the elders remembered how the British had avenged the deaths at Chief Willy Tom Robins funeral by burning down the original village. Mary had to explain that that act by the British was wrong. Many innocent people were punished. Because of her impending trip Mary's popularity with the villagers of Old Town was more evident than ever. Efiks that she thought were unaffected by the Gospel now came to her to urge caution, their eyes wide with concern. Women confined to yards begged that she come to them to say good-bye. They hugged her and cried. Never had she felt so much like a "White Ma." Never had she known such warmth and joy. She felt a very loved part of an enormous family.

"But I mustn't react with pride," she had to remind herself. "This opportunity is God's doing, not mine."

It became even more difficult not to feel pride when the king's great canoe arrived. The English word *canoe* was inadequate; the long, hollowed-out vessel held forty people! A cannon mounted on the bow glinted its brass like gold in the sun. The sides of the boat had been freshly painted in bright colors. Mary's own space in the boat was protected by an enclosed structure of mats. Bags of rice being sent to Okon as a gift were arranged into a couch for her. Although departure had been scheduled for nine o'clock in the morning Mary was delayed by still more villagers saying good-bye and urging caution. Wise in their ways, she set about preparing the evening meal. The farewells took hours. It was late in the evening before the boat was able to depart.

"Sio uden!" barked the coxswain.

The canoe sped away as thirty-three men dug oars into the river. They paddled to the coxswain's drum beat. The canoe surged down the river. The men began to sing songs.

"Our lovely *Ma Akamba* we bear," the oarsmen sang. "Row! Row! Row!"

Inside her hut Mary was embarrassed. Such undeserved praise the men gave her. She set her jaws, so as to not show her bairns how pleased she was. But the children could not see her in the candlelight because they were all fast asleep. The river was calm this night. She had tried not to think about the actual journey.

This was no simple river trip. That was one of the reasons King Eyo Honesty had insisted on the use of his vessel. This trip was across the great estuary where it was many miles wide. In a storm this trip would be like canoeing a raging sea. But there was no storm tonight. Praise God, the water of the estuary must have been as smooth as glass. Mary finally slept herself. The late departure wasn't so bad after all, if one could sleep the night on a gentle river.

"Our lovely *Ma Akamba* is at Ibaka!" called the coxswain, waking Mary from her sleep many hours later.

Mary peeked out of the enclosure. The jungle beyond the narrow sandy beach was serene in early morning light. The oarsmen, tired as they were, eagerly carried her and the children into Ibaka. There the level of interest was even higher than it had been in Old Town. The Efiks swarmed around her.

Intense interest was an anathema to Mary. She was never more content than when she was allowed to serve Christ without notice. But this barrier with these Efiks who had never seen a white person before had to be crossed. So she smiled as sweetly as she could.

"Welcome to Ibaka!" boomed a voice. It was the chief. Okon sat on chair, winged on each side by his subchiefs. Because of his remoteness, Okon was not as Anglicized as many Efik chiefs, but still he wore a top hat and pinstriped trousers under a leopard skin robe. "This woman will do many great things for us," he bellowed proudly. Then he stared at Mary expectantly.

"Friends," Mary shouted, raising her arms, "I have come to tell you of a Savior. If you believe in Him, He will save you from death." Mary noted their stony disbelief and continued, "I will also give you the white man's medicine. You can come to me with your sickness." Murmurs of enthusiasm rippled. "I will teach you how to keep yourselves and your babies clean and prevent sickness." More approval. "I will teach you to make clothing and wash it." A smattering of accord. "Thank you for coming to see me," she concluded.

The chief could not subdue the crowd. His welcome and her promise to them had released their inhibitions. They surrounded her. She allowed them to poke at her, though she rebuked those who were too rough. Fingers tested her flaming hair. Hands felt the cloth of her dress. A few touched her skin cautiously.

"She is not painted," one gasped.

A thumb scoured her freckles. "They don't rub off," said the prober.

They sniffed at her.

This curiosity continued for hours. At lunch they watched her eat, their own jaws agape. Those in the front of the crowd screamed to the ones behind.

"She's scooping the black soup into her mouth with a shiny tool!"

"She's picking the bones out of the fish with a pronged tool!"

"She's touching her mouth with a cloth!"

After lunch Mary indulged latecomers and a handful who had to be dragged before her. The fearful she tried to calm.

"Come to your lodging," announced the chief finally.

Mary and her bairns were installed in the chief's "yard," the compound for his wives and young children. The chief also kept his goats, chickens, and dogs there. Mary resented the perception of the chief's minions that she, too, was a possession of the chief. But no other accommodation was available, and the yard was well guarded. Moreover, Mary was placed in a special hut, modesty assured by a curtain of calico hung over the door.

But any pleasure in her special status disappeared the first night. Mary discovered that the wives, all prodigiously fat and smeared with palm oil, had to observe proper etiquette for a guest. This was shown by sleeping as snug to her as possible. So in the hut Mary was hemmed in on all sides by the chief's very large, oily wives, all of whom exuded the smell of palm oil and perspiration.

After dark Mary asked, "Would someone please raise the curtain over the door?" She added with conviction, "A breeze would be nice."

The next day she began her doctoring. Unless it was Sunday, this was always the first thing to be done. It had been no different with Livingstone. Many of the natives were suffering, often in the depths of depression with worry. She could not keep them waiting. Infections were common. Mary cleaned, disinfected, and bandaged the wounds. She had powders suitable for stomach problems and headaches. She had medicine for diarrhea. She had quinine for jungle fever. A few severe illnesses, especially those caused by parasites, she could do nothing more than diagnose. But this was helpful to the suffering too.

"It is up to you to transport the patient to Duke Town for medical attention," Mary would tell Chief Okon. "It is your duty as a good chief who cares for his people."

After the medical emergencies were handled Mary began holding church services, morning and evening. It was important to observe a dignified, formal ritual. This was the most serious business of all. She herself made every effort to be neat and wear clean clothes. All her helpers were also spotless. On a table Mary spread a white cloth, then the Bible and the cross. The crowds to hear the story of Jesus and salvation were very large. Chief Okon was there, flying the colors for Jesus, too. Mary had to shout to reach the far edge of the crowd. She soon learned many had come from smaller villages back in the jungle. They begged her to come with them to their villages.

"You must not go back in the jungle," warned Chief Okon. "This is elephant country. They are everywhere. Only a handful of Efiks manage to protect their farms from the elephants in this country. The rest of us fish in the river and the sea for our livelihood."

But one day Mary did go back into the jungle because elephants were reported across a lagoon where they would not be dangerous to her. Still, she made the four bairns stay in the village. It seemed a dream to be watching the great gray beasts splash in the water and trumpet ear-splitting warnings. She no longer wondered how a herd of elephants could destroy a tiny farm in minutes! And she silently praised God there were no elephants in the Efik country east of the Cross River.

Back in Ibaka the village had erupted in a search for a python! A child had seen the great snake and now everyone hunted it. The men waved machetes. A few brandished old rusty muskets foisted on them by Efik traders. Mary rushed to the compound to make sure her four bairns were all right. Then she looked around for the snake like everyone else. The treacherous constrictor was never found. It made Mary realize how primeval and vulnerable this village was. Evidence of primitive human practices was everywhere too. Skulls dangled on the tops of poles. Tiny devil huts here and there were stocked with food to appease evil spirits. Mary knew these Efiks also practiced slavery and probably twin murder and human sacrifice too.

"Men and women still carry the original sin," said Mary. "I must give them good hearts through Christ."

Jungle fever struck Mary. *Physician, heal thyself!* she told herself. For two days she fought it with quinine.

And the fever subsided. But not the crush of problems in Ibaka. The next morning Mary found herself in the center of a human storm. Two young wives had sneaked out of the yard to visit a young man. But they were seen. Soon it was discovered that two other wives in the yard had known they had left and said nothing. They, too, were in trouble. The four were being held for punishment.

"This is very bad," said Chief Okon. "A wife must remain pure." He looked at Mary for a reaction.

How could she argue with what he said?

He continued, "Other wives must not pretend to be ignorant of such a great crime."

"What punishment do you plan?" asked Mary cautiously.

"I have already met with the elders. One hundred lashes with the whip of crocodile hide!"

"That's too much!" said Mary angrily.

"But the four wives must be flogged. If you stop it with your written Word of God, the people will say your way is no good because it destroys our power to punish wrongdoers."

Such severe punishment made Mary cringe. She was no stranger to such proceedings. Not only was the flogging unimaginably painful, but salt was rubbed into the wounds afterwards. And sometimes those who administered the violent justice got carried away and cut off a finger or two for good measure!

"We need a big palaver," she told Chief Okon, looking stern but reasonable.

She couldn't believe she was acting so boldly. Years ago she would have done everything in her power to work the punishment out behind the scenes. She was terrified of men. But now she felt so bold and so authoritative through Christ's strength that she was willing to take on all the men and their system of justice in front of the entire village! Yes, surely the power of Christ worked through her. She seemed to be carried along by a tide. After Chief Okon had gathered the elders and the four wives, it was Mary who stepped before the entire assemblage. Carrying the Bible, she directed an icy stare at the four plump, very young wives.

"You wives have shamed all the women of the village with your foolishness!" she snapped. The wives seemed stunned. "Wives must remain pure," she continued. "You betrayed your chief's confidence. You must pray to the one true God above that He will protect you in the future from temptation. The Word of God I bring you in this sacred book says that God has mercy."

The four wives began to relax; surely the White Ma was going to let them go unpunished after all.

Mary continued, "But God does not overlook sin, nor does God forbid punishment for sin."

The wives looked sick.

"Now she speaks well," grunted an elder.

Mary turned on the elders, "It is your terrible system of taking many wives that causes these young women to get bored and stray. Men should not have more than one wife!"

"Huh?" blurted Chief Okon. "Did I hear the White Ma right? What's this about not having more than one wife?"

"It's a shame to pen these young women up like animals," she said to the chief.

"Does it say that in your book?" yelled the chief.

"Right here in the tenth chapter of Mark," she cried. "It says a man shall leave his father and mother, and cleave to his wife. And the two shall be one flesh. And he may not put that wife away and take another, or it is great sin against the first wife!"

Chief Okon was boiling. "I don't know about this Word of God. . . ."

An elder growled, "Are these sinful wives not to be punished after all?"

Another added, "This new way of the White Ma is not good."

"Listen to me!" Mary held up her hand. "The wives must be punished for their foolishness. The hide of the crocodile is appropriate. . . ."

"She speaks wisdom now!" yelled an elder.

"No salt in the wounds," she insisted.

"Granted," commented the chief.

"No fingers or toes may be cut off," added Mary.

"That's a small thing anyway," shrugged an elder.

Mary announced, "Each wife should get ten lashes!"

"Only ten?" gasped an elder.

She appealed to Chief Okon. "Why would you want to scar your beautiful young wives any more than necessary?"

Arguing began. Mary stood her ground. Finally the elders agreed. "Ten lashes is almost as painful as a hundred lashes," commented one elder matter-of-factly. "After the first ten lashes they usually faint anyway."

There was nothing for Mary to do then but pray for the wives and wait. One by one the overweight wives stumbled back into the compound, sobbing and breathless. They flopped on their stomachs, their blubbery backs striped with blood. Mary cleaned their wounds, rubbed in an analgesic salve, and gave them an opiate. Eventually the four sobbed themselves to sleep. She would keep them sedated for a day or two—at least until the worst part of the pain was over.

Soon after that incident she had to leave for Old Town. She had agreed to stay only fourteen days. "Are you going with us?" she asked Chief Okon when she loaded her belongings into the great canoe the evening of the departure.

"Yes, White Ma."

Mary was pleased. It meant Chief Okon held no resentment over the confrontation about the wives. He was forgiving, even pliable. Mary climbed in and made sure her four bairns were comfortable. It was already almost dark, so the chief ordered a pot of yams and herbs be put on board. All of them would eat en route. The water was a sheet of glass. The oarsmen took turns eating as they cruised out into the great estuary.

After an hour or so the boat began to surge in great bursts. Mary peeked out of the mat enclosure to see the crewmen rowing furiously. Chief Okon grimly pointed to the northeastern sky. The sky was very dark, but wasn't it dusk anyway?

"Big wind coming," said Chief Okon.

"Tornado?" she asked the chief, using the local name for the ferocious line squalls. "This late in the day?"

"It happens once in a while."

"We should turn back."

"It's too late. We'll be blown right out to sea. We must get to that island."

Mary squinted ahead. The chief had the eyes of a

cat. She didn't see any island. Still, if there was an island perhaps they would be safe on the lee side of it. But was there an island? The oarsmen continued to row madly. No one wanted to be caught out in the great estuary in a storm. Suddenly wind slapped her face!

"Tornado," she gasped.

Now the oarsmen really fought the estuary. The surface was no longer calm but kicking up into waves three and four feet high. Mary prayed. *O God spare us. We have so much to do yet. But do Your will.* She prayed and prayed. She thanked God for his infinite goodness. She thanked God for her wonderful life. Outside the enclosure she could see nothing in the maelstrom raging around her. Surely they were being driven out to sea!

"Grab hold, men!" yelled the chief.

What did Chief Okon mean? Mary peeked out of the enclosure and strained to see. It seemed the men were half standing in the canoe. Her face was thrashed by leaves. Then she realized they had made it to the island. But not onto a beach. They had rowed into a watery thicket of bushes and now they clung to the branches. It was none too soon as she felt water rising up over her feet, then above her ankles. She kept checking on her four bairns as the vessel rocked in the howling wind. Suddenly the sky flashed lightning. She and her bairns were no longer inside an enclosure. The mats had blown away. The rain stung her cheeks. She was chilled. Then she felt as if she were covered with ice. Soon she ached as if her bones were frozen solid. Surely an attack of malaria was coinciding with the drenching from the storm. She certainly could not treat herself with quinine now.

"The big wind is almost gone," yelled Chief Okon.

Mary thanked God for his mercy. In a few minutes all was serene. Ridiculously so, it seemed to Mary, after such a killer storm. Now, except for a few sprinkles, the water was like glass again.

The oarsmen bailed the water out of the vessel, singing all the while. Then the men rowed away from the lee side of the island and plowed toward Old Town to the beat of their coxswain's drum.

At dawn they cruised up the Calabar River to Old Town. Mary was so sick she had to be carried to her mission hut. But she was very pleased to see her bairns, especially the new baby Janie, were fine. Now all she had to do when she felt better was to check on Janie's twin brother, Robby.

NINE

K eep a close eye on these bairns," Mary told her assistant.

Her assistant tried to keep her in the hut that very first evening, but Mary had to see the twin, Robby. Burning in the early stages of the fever that followed the chills, Mary stumbled toward the house of Yaba, the friend who cared for Robby. Getting to Yaba's hut was no simple matter. The people of Old Town were over-joyed to see her, and she seemed to be delayed every step of the way. Mary had held church services in the chief's yard as always, and she had told the villagers about her adventures in Ibaka, but they had to know more. The fact that Yaba had not been at the service did not bother her. After all it was difficult to leave a tiny baby.

Finally she poked her head in her friend Yaba's hut. "Greetings," she said as cheerfully as possible. Yaba eased past her into the yard. She was clutching a baby too old to be Robby. The baby was her own. Mary tried to calm her own rising fear. "Where is Robby?"

"Gone with relatives." Yaba was very nervous.

"Relatives?"

"Several men came. . . ."

"Egbo?"

"No. One of them said the baby surely had to be the baby of his nephew's wife, and he wanted to take care of the boy."

Mary felt as if she would collapse. Somehow word leaked out that Yaba was caring for a new infant. Yaba's own infant was too young. Someone must have figured out the new infant could not be hers. Someone must have guessed the twins in the clay pot had been found. Mary's head was swimming with fever. The whole thing was horrifying. She could not blame Yaba in any way. Yaba was only trying to help. Would the villains now come after Janie?

"Did you know the man who took Robby?" asked Mary weakly.

"No, but I think they were from somewhere up-river. . . ."

"Upriver," repeated Mary dully, remembering the trader had found the clay pot upriver.

Surely Robby was dead by now. The villains wouldn't just abandon the infant as they had the first time. Mary returned to her hut, barely able to walk. After all the near disasters on her trip to and from Ibaka, she returned to a tragedy right in her backyard! She took to bed and nursed herself with quinine. She resolved to speak out more and more about twins. She must change the hearts of the Efiks. Twins were not the offspring of demons. Surely in time the Efiks could be convinced.

"After all," she mumbled in her fever, "many tribes west of the Cross River, I heard, prize twins."

The next months were grim for Mary. No sooner had she recovered from her jungle fever than the worst tornado she had witnessed since she came to Africa hammered Old Town. It ripped the roof off her hut and crumpled one wall. She kept her operation going only because a good man offered her space in the little building by the river that housed his palm-oil factory.

The next visit by Daddy Anderson was eventful.

"Good Lord, Mary!" he exclaimed. "You look like a ghost."

"We've had a run of bad luck here," she sighed.

"You've been here since late '80 without a furlough."

Late 1880? Yes, that seemed right to her. Although things were getting harder to remember. And what was today? Sometime in 1883? Yes, that seemed right. Late 1880 to sometime in 1883. How long was that? Two years? Three years? It was so hard for her to think these days. Since Robby's disappearance her thoughts had been muddled. But that was due to the sickness at Ihaka, too, probably. Then the terrible storm came. And now she was here in this factory building. . . .

"Are you all right, Mary?" asked Daddy Anderson.

"Just doing my mathematics. I figure I'm not due for another furlough for a good while."

"We have rules for that, but we don't abandon our common sense, Mary."

"Are you suggesting I return to Scotland?"

"I'm ordering it."

"Only if I can take Janie with me."

"Janie?"

"Yes, my baby Janie."

She couldn't leave Janie behind. She had left Robby behind. No, Janie must go with her to Scotland.

Daddy Anderson insisted Mary come to Mission Hill above Duke Town to await the steamer to England. Janie was allowed to come, too. At Mission Hill Mary rested. Days later she was not improved with rest, but had to be carried aboard the ship. She heard whispers worrying whether she would survive the voyage. Her life was in God's hands, as it always was.

God restored her strength on the voyage. By the time she arrived in Downfield, the country village near Dundee where she had moved her mother and sisters, she was eager to have Janie baptized. Somehow she had never managed to have Janie baptized in Calabar. The lack of ordained Christian ministers to perform baptism and holy communion for the flock around Calabar gnawed at Mary, but now in the summer of 1883 she was back in Scotland with her chance to recruit good people for Calabar, wasn't she? And with this great need buoying her she fought her old dread of speaking in public.

"But first Janie will be baptized in the Presbyterian Church of Scotland," she declared.

Then, with the African child Janie at her side, Mary delivered her message to her audiences: The heathen did not need self-righteousness, patronage, and pity. In fact they resented these attitudes. All they wanted were refinement and education; they sensed they were ignorant of some very important things. Emotions shown them by missionaries should be only sympathy and patience. And the education must be in depth, with full instruction in the Bible, too, not just special passages selected for the purposes of evangelism. The heathen were hungry for instruction, but they must not be shortchanged!

And in a stinging rebuke she pointed out how shallow the religious instruction had become for children in Scotland. "So little depth! Children can't be nourished in Christ by a few platitudes."

Mary soon realized workers in the church, not just in Edinburgh and Dundee either, were becoming very much aware of her. Youths, especially younger women who dreamed of similar pursuits for Christ, held her in awe. While Mary stayed in Edinburgh a young lady named Jessie Hogg was introduced to her. Jessie taught children in a mission sponsored by the Bristo Street church.

"I so admire what you are doing in Africa," Jessie told Mary breezily. "If only I could do that."

"Then what keeps you from doing it?" asked Mary bluntly.

"Why, nothing I suppose," was Jessie's halting answer.

"Then come to Calabar."

"But. . ."

"But, nothing. Apply to the Foreign Mission Board straightaway."

With that prompting Jessie Hogg did apply. And it seemed just days later Jessie was starting several weeks of medical training before leaving for Calabar! She discovered that she would journey to Africa even before Mary would return. Jessie Hogg had found out, as people found out in earlier times with David Livingstone, that good intentions were not enough. Good intentions yes, but then action!

Action became a double-edged sword for Mary, too. Her speaking in public, fearful though it might have been, was so well received that the ladies of Glasgow prevailed upon the foreign mission authorities to keep Mary in Scotland on a speaking circuit. She was upset by this because by late 1884 she had already received approval to return to her beloved Old Town. But how could she refute their reasoning? Hadn't she recruited Jessie Hogg in the twinkling of an eye? Think of all the young ladies she might influence to go to Africa, argued the authorities. And so Mary began speaking, still with agonizing difficulty if men were present, all around Scotland. Days became weeks. Weeks became months. Instead of returning to Africa in early 1884 as she had planned she was still in Scotland in late 1884!

"You must go to Creek Town on your return," James Logie told an astonished Mary. "Miss Johnstone, who currently teaches there, is losing her health."

This news, which denied her return to Old Town, did not cheer Mary. But she knew all too well how one could lose her health in Africa. And the mission at Creek Town, the abode of their most powerful Efik ally, King Eyo Honesty, was too important not to fully staff.

Then Mary's own family in Downfield started to lose their health. First it was mother, not so unexpected as she neared the age of seventy. But Mary was not prepared for her youngest sister Jane's deterioration as winter set in. Jane complained bitterly of the cold. A physician suggested a milder climate.

"You must go to Africa with me," Mary told her sister.

"Africa!"

Mary appealed to the Foreign Mission Board to let her take her sister Jane back to Creek Town with her. Otherwise she would not feel free to leave Scotland at all. The commissioners resisted her appeal. Take an invalid to Africa? Surely there must be a better solution, they insisted. But what?

"Perhaps I should not return to Africa," she told her mother.

Her mother shook her head. "You were given to me by God, Mary. I gave you back to God years ago. You must go where He needs you."

But her mother's willingness to let her return to Africa did not solve the problems in Scotland. What could be done about sister Jane? Mary prayed and prayed until her prayer was answered. A Presbyterian woman in Exeter, about as far south in England as one could live, suggested Mary move her family there. But was Exeter so warm? Mary sought advice from Foreign Mission Board commissioners. They were enthusiastic. Oh yes, the climate of southern England was much milder than Scotland. Granted it might snow there a few days during the winter. And it did freeze on the coldest nights in January, but southern England did not suffer the long durations of cold that Scotland suffered.

"But where would my family live?" asked Mary, still much in doubt.

Her receptiveness triggered activity in Exeter. Soon Mr. Ellis, a deacon in the Congregational Church, had found a house for the family in the village of Topsham.

Almost in a daze Mary found herself once again moving her family. Sister Susan temporarily remained in Scotland, visiting friends. It seemed that no sooner had the family settled in Topsham that they received the crushing news Susan had abruptly died! The poor woman had been visiting Mr. Martin's married daughter, Mrs. M'Crindle, in Edinburgh. Mary was stunned. Sister Susan? And all their worry had been over sister Jane? But Mary had to have courage. This tragedy might harm both sister Jane and her mother.

Soon after Susan's death her mother's health did worsen. "Now what must I do?" Mary asked God. "Sister Jane is too weak to care for mother."

In the back of her mind Mary fought growing anger and frustration. She had been away from Calabar for over two years now. She seemed mired in quicksand. Was she ever going to get out? What was she going to do? She couldn't leave her family. Not now. As always she prayed.

Suddenly she remembered an old acquaintance in Dundee. The friend was about her age and reliable. Mary had worked with her in the factory. It was over ten years ago, Mary realized with a start. Nevertheless, Mary had heard the woman was still unmarried.

Mary poured out her heart in a letter. Oh, she was asking so much of her friend. But could she come to Topsham and take care of her family while Mary was in Africa?

"Now we can only wait," she told her African child Janie.

Janie was a constant reminder of how long Mary had floundered in Scotland and England. Upon their arrival Janie was a babbling infant in diapers. Now she toddled about in dresses and spoke English! That, too, jolted Mary. She had to get Janie back to her people.

"Praise God for His mercy," cried Mary when the letter came from Scotland. "My friend is coming."

Assured of her family's care, Mary departed from England with the toddler Janie in November 1885. But she was not serene. There had been a haunting sense of finality in their farewells. The poor health of her mother and her sister weighed on her mind all the time. Would Mary ever be able to open a letter from England again without fearing the worst? She fought against becoming morbid. One could not truly trust God and harbor such doubt. So she read her Bible every spare moment on the voyage. Surely back in Creek Town her work for Christ would erase all worries. By New Year's Eve she and Janie were back in Creek Town. To forestall the European custom of swilling alcohol to celebrate the coming new year Mary gathered her young Efik men together to pray and sing hymns. Reverend Luke, due to go upriver soon with his wife to one of the outposts, read Psalm 90. The opening verses, so choked with sorrow and regret, were followed by sunshiny verses of hope:

So teach us to number our days,
that we may apply our hearts unto wisdom.
Return, O LORD, how long?
and let it repent thee concerning thy servants.
O satisfy us early with thy mercy;
that we may rejoice and be glad all our days.
Make us glad according to the days wherein
thou hast afflicted us, and the years wherein we
have seen evil.

Let thy work appear unto thy servants, and thy glory unto their children.

And let the beauty of the LORD our God be upon us: and establish thou the work of our hands upon us; yea, the work of our hands establish thou it.

Work as she did Mary could not escape the dread she felt about her mother and sister. Every letter worried her. Weeping often overcame her. And she wept for many minutes at a time.

Was this prophetic? Yes. Within weeks of the New Year Mary received the awful news: Mother had died. The letter assured her that Mother had died in loving hands. She was laid to rest in the cemetery of the Congregational Church in Topsham. Mary put the letter aside and that very night conducted a prayer meeting in Creek Town, not as if nothing happened, but with a heart broken. Later she wrote to ask her sister Jane for more details of Mother's last hours and for a keepsake.

"Just a little something to look at," she wrote in her letter to Topsham.

Meanwhile she toiled at Creek Town with two other ladies, Miss Edgerly and the ailing Miss Johnstone. Reverend Goldie was now the ordained pastor there. Mary helped run the Goldies' household, where she lodged. She taught Sunday school, regular school, and Bible lessons to the native children. She taught native women how to care for babies. The child Janie, now very spoiled, kept Mary busy, too. And then came the one development regarding Janie that Mary had always dreaded.

An Efik man presented himself to her one day in

Creek Town. "That child over there you call 'Janie' is my daughter."

Mary rebuked him for the disappearance of her twin brother "Robby." As he denied having anything to do with that incident, Mary searched his eyes. She also remembered Yaba saying it was this man's uncle who took Robby.

"Why are you here now?" she asked, finally knowing in her heart that this man had nothing to do with Robby's disappearance.

"I want only to look at her from a distance."

"You will do no such thing!"

Mary pulled him toward Janie. Janie was petrified at the towering man. The man stood there as if in a stupor. Mary forced father and daughter to embrace. All barriers crumbled. Within minutes the two seemed inseparable. The man promised to return often and to bring food. He kept his promise, too, bringing his wife. To her unutterable sorrow Mary learned this wife was not the mother of Janie. That mother had been killed by the villagers. Yet, again in her heart Mary felt the father was not responsible for that tragedy.

"He, too, is surely a victim of the devilish beliefs about twins," she said. "I can see the pain in his eyes."

Mary could never turn down an orphan. Besides Janie, who slept in Mary's bed, she mothered a six-year-old girl, every bit as active as Janie. And there was Okin, a boy of eight, given to Mary not by his mother, who was a slave and had no voice in his upbringing, but by the mother's mistress! She insisted the boy be raised a Christian. What convoluted relationships, lamented Mary. But she must not let the boy suffer, although the way Okin destroyed his clothes made her want to renege once or twice. Also among her bairns was Ekim, the son of the main chief of Old Town. He was a freeman, possible heir to Old Town, and an important charge. Not last or least was thirteen-year-old Inyang, a very large, good-hearted girl who helped Mary. And of course, Mary could not turn down five-month-old twins found discarded. Nor could she turn away another young child—Annie—who was believed cursed. The child's deceased mother had been a slave to one of King Eyo Honesty's daughters, who had none of her father's goodness.

When Mary asked the king's daughter if one of her other slaves might help care for the child, the daughter snarled, "Let the child die!"

Swamped by such responsibilities on top of all her teaching duties, Mary had little time to dwell on the death of her mother. And if such a rare moment of pause came to her it was usually interrupted by the appearance of a sick person needing medical attention. And that taken care of, Mary felt a definite responsibility to visit native women in their yards. These poor confined souls needed attention, too. One poor woman was blind. Never was there a poor soul more helpless. Her hut was a shambles. She was completely dependent on others. Yet, the gospel gave her a joy few other people possessed. She sang all day long like a lark. No one could grumble or groan after hearing her.

Even King Eyo Honesty marveled. "Look at what Christ's love has done for that poor woman."

Such was the mountain of activity demanded of Mary. Whether Mary liked it or not she had little time to mourn for her mother, even when Jane sent her mother's tiny worn wedding ring as a keepsake. Then came the next blow.

"Sister Jane is dead!" she cried after opening a letter in the spring of 1886. "She's resting beside Mother now."

Never had Mary felt so abandoned. England and Scotland held nothing for her now. For her, life without torment was possible only during activity that absorbed all of her. For if she paused to reflect for one moment, the memories of the deaths of her mother and sisters stung her like angry hornets. How she had planned for them! Moved them and their belongings. Written letters. Prevailed on old friends. Had she been a fool? How could God do this to her? She scolded herself. She was nothing. God's will was everything. But the memories were bitter. And whom was there anywhere in the world she wanted to write of her African triumphs and trials? No one. All dead.

"Heaven is closer to me now than England and Scotland," she said bitterly.

But surely hope had to triumph over despair. Could she turn the demise of her entire family into something good for Christ? No longer could the excuse of a family that depended on her in Britain be used to prevent her from penetrating the wildest parts of Africa! Perhaps there was a new way to accomplish that goal. Hadn't James Logie told her back in 1881 or so that the missionary women were going to have more freedom to choose when their auxiliary was approved by the Foreign Mission Board? And hadn't the concept of the women's "Zenana Mission Committee" been approved the following year? And hadn't the ladies formed the Zenana Mission Committee for Calabar in May of 1886?

"So, first I will go about convincing the ladies of the Zenana Mission Committee to approve my plan," she reasoned.

The men of the local mission committee gasped at the proposal by the auxiliary several weeks later. "Send Mary Slessor among the Okoyong? The meanest, most primitive tribe we know? Why, she must go up the Calabar River. There's no civilization on that river beyond Creek Town itself. Perhaps we could send her to one of our newer outposts along the Cross River. Oh, and we mustn't forget that Miss Edgerly and Miss Johnstone are returning to Scotland on furlough. Heavens, how could the mission at Creek Town spare Miss Slessor, anyway?"

But they found the auxiliary as determined as Mary. Mary had reasoned correctly, too. Once the argument that her family in Britain depended on her was removed, the mission committee's objections sputtered out. Who had learned Efik better than Mary? Who had handled the Efiks better than Mary? The committee had to admit she was held in awe by nearly everyone, including King Eyo Honesty. Kings and chiefs all over the immediate Calabar region had requested her services. The ruling Efiks seemed almost to fear her. And yet she was tender to the tiniest infant.

The local mission committee could not refuse her out of hand.

Mary definitely possessed some special gift from God that few other missionaries had. "Yes, God might well have His finger on this," some of them whispered. Perhaps it was best not to interfere. Did any of them want to be immortalized as short-sighted fools like the handful who opposed the great Livingstone? And yet, what would the world think of cads who sent such a tiny woman to the most savage people on the face of the earth? What if she were murdered?

One day in October 1886 one of the missionaries in Creek Town approached Mary with a most confounded look on his face. "I have official news for you from the mission committee. . . ."

TEN

"They have approved my mission to the Okoyong!" guessed Mary.

"Yes."

Accompanied by several of the male missionaries, she met with the Okoyong tribesmen up the Cross River near Iknetu. She was startled. The Okoyong differed physically from the Efiks. The Okoyong were taller and finer featured. At this first palaver with Mary the glowering chiefs scarcely spoke to her or any of the missionaries.

"Promise you missionaries that a little woman can live among us in peace?" one finally growled. "Unthinkable!"

The Okoyong chiefs were still glowering when the missionaries broke off the first palaver. Mary fought disappointment. How often had she dreamed of ministering among these wildest of tribes? A thousand times. And now it might not be possible at all.

One thing was certain. She had much to learn about them. For some reason she had thought they were Efiks, but wilder. But now it seemed they were some separate tribe. Their language was similar but distinct from Efik. One missionary said it sounded like the "Bantu" widely spoken by tribes in the Cameroons and farther south. Indeed, rumors said the Okoyong were an extension of peoples from the south. Did this mean the Okoyong might not practice the same abominations—twin killing, human sacrifice—that had almost been eradicated in the Efiks nearest Calabar? Would their practices be less brutal—or more? One could not help but note their absolute ferocity. And it had not been that long ago that the Okoyong had kidnapped one of the missionaries and demanded rum and gin and guns for his ransom!

Of course Mary insisted on meeting the tribesmen again. *Yes, the Okoyong will be a great challenge,* she bolstered herself.

To her delight the other missionaries were just as determined as she was. But the second palaver many months later failed, too. Were the Okoyong savages impenetrable? Each meeting was arranged only through what seemed interminable intrigue.

Still, the third palaver in early 1888 seemed to succeed. "Why would great warriors of the Okoyong fear a tiny little woman?" argued one shrewd missionary.

"Yes then," answered one of the chiefs testily, "the little woman can go to Ekenge in the very heart of the Okoyong!" But the way there was not from the Cross River, Mary learned. Ekenge was reached from the Calabar River. There was just enough doubt about the chiefs' sincerity to send chills up and down Mary's back. Was it possible the chief at Ekenge knew nothing of her coming?

Nevertheless back at Creek Town Mary set about immediately to prepare for her first real foray among the Okoyong. "Praise God for this opportunity," she told anyone who would listen. "It is His doing."

"I can't praise God for this," blurted one of her students. "You are going to your death!"

Once again King Eyo Honesty made his canoe available to her. She sat on cushions within a small curtained enclosure. Her only provisions for this trip were bread, canned stew, tea, a small paraffin stove, and plenty of prayer. With the familiar coxswain and his powerful oarsmen she traveled up the Calabar River in the king's canoe. On the Cross River she would not have been nearly as far north as the mission of Ikorofiong, but on the Calabar River she was in territory almost untouched by any travelers other than Okoyong. The canoe stopped at a path abutting the river bank. This was reputed to be the way to the village of Ekenge. The king's crewmen looked very relieved they were not going with her.

Mary had other plans. "King Eyo Honesty would desire that several of you go with me," she said abruptly.

With the crewmen the coxswain selected, she plunged into the very wilds of Okoyong. The rain forest here was like the forest she had known in the Old Town area. It was not an impenetrable tangle of jungle growth at all. It, too, was dominated by trees of many species, typically branchless below their crowns. A dense canopy of leaves rustled about 60 feet overhead. By now Mary knew that another tier of crowns topped out at about 120 feet, but the canopy was not as dense. And she had been told there was even a third tier of crowns, least dense of all, at a dizzying height of about 200 feet.

Vines and undergrowth grew in abundance, but on an established path one could easily walk through such a forest. Four miles into this rain forest, which Mary considered quite benign as long as one wasn't foolish, was supposedly the village of Ekenge.

"Yes, there is a village ahead," she cried after an hour of walking.

Suddenly several warriors blocked the path. "Where are you going?" they asked.

"I have been invited to Ekenge," she answered in their language. She had picked up the rudiments during the palavers.

"We shall see. This way."

The warriors led Mary and her companions along a secondary path to a clearing. There their chief lived in what passed for Okoyong splendor. His large mud hut was in the center of the extensive clearing.

"But where is Ekenge?" Mary asked the warrior who did all the talking.

"Beyond!" snorted the warrior. "Do you not know chiefs must live apart?"

"But why?"

"Why?" he gasped. "For protection. A chief can trust no one. He must sleep with his guns and machetes at his side. Just as every man must sleep with weapons at his side."

Mary was presented to Chief Edem, who was flanked on both sides by dozens of his court. "I have come from down the river," she said. "I bring you the promise of better things to come."

"We shall see," he said.

His calmness told Mary he expected her. He blinked

though. Was he surprised she came after all? Or was he surprised such a small woman was so noisy? Maybe he was surprised by everything about her: her ghostly skin, her flaming hair, her cool blue eyes, her confident manner, her courage—or was it foolishness? Pleased that he was sober and that apparently he knew she was coming, she continued in a confident vein about the glories that awaited the Okoyong.

One woman beside him seemed especially prominent in his court. Not only was she the epitome of Okoyong womanhood, with enormous bulk, but her comments were articulate, soothing. Other remarks revealed she was not the chief's wife but his sister, Eme Ete. Mary began watching the sister's reaction to her own comments to the chief. It seemed a good gauge of how a suggestion might be affecting him. The chief himself maintained a stony look. And he had not yet extended an invitation to Mary to stay in Ekenge.

Finally Mary said, "I hear the village of Ifako is near here." Eme Ete, the chief's sister, raised an eyebrow in appreciation. Mary continued, "I wish to visit there."

"The chief there is probably as drunk as a monkey!" snapped Chief Edem. "A white woman will not like it there. You stay in Ekenge."

"I would like to tell you more about Jesus now."

So Mary told the natives of Ekenge how much God loved them. He loved them so much He sent His only Son to die for them. He had ransomed them for eternity. If only the chief would let her stay in Ekenge a long while, she would teach them how to come to Jesus. Their lives would be immeasurably better.

The chief remained stern but attentive. It was his

sister Eme Ete who finally silenced Mary by taking her arm while smiling ever so slightly, probably still appreciating how Mary triggered the chief's jealousy into an invitation to stay.

"Come with me," Eme Ete said quietly.

She led Mary to a yard guarded by warriors. Mary's crewmen idled nervously outside the yard. Inside the yard lived several of the chief's wives and one infant. Also in the yard milled chickens, goats, dogs, and two specimens of a scrawny kind of short-horned cow found in the lowland jungles. Like anyone who had ever read David Livingstone's exploits, Mary knew the sad state of livestock in the jungle areas was due to the scourge of the tsetse fly. All concerned would have liked fat cows and sturdy horses, but these animals could not survive the tsetse fly. Only this gaunt kind of cow called a "muturu" survived the lowland jungles. No one knew why.

Eme Ete saw that all the visitors were fed. And Mary soon realized the variety and abundance served was meant to be proof that Chief Edem's people did not want for food. What was not obvious was explained by Eme Ete. She waved at nearby clearings. These Okoyong too knew the value of palm oil, so areas had been cleared to allow sunshine to nourish the oil palms. The clearings allowed other sun-loving crops to grow too, explained Eme Ete, especially corn and yams and plantains, a kind of cooking banana. Mary was surprised to see cocoyams served. It was the first she knew this recent import from South America was reaching the interior beyond the main trading areas.

"Fufu," commented Mary as she tried mashed manioc.

Eme Ete shrugged indifference. Because of a preponderance of shade, the manioc was the only vegetable that grew in the jungle with little trouble. In its many forms it was probably the staple of the Okoyong diet. Mary didn't believe natives other than the king and his court enjoyed the variety she was being offered. The manioc had to be boiled first to remove its acid. Then after being peeled it was fried; or it was mashed as fufu; or it was ground into flour to make patties. But was their monotonous diet so different from the potato-eating Irish or the porridge-slurping Scots? Meat was in some of the offerings this day, and Mary did not want to know its origin, for she knew only too well the natives ate "bush meat": flesh of any creature—four legged, six legged, eight legged, or none—they could spear or snare or club. Fish was probably common fare here as it was all along the river. There seemed no alcohol in any form. Were they too isolated to have the white man's poison, rum and gin? Did they not even drink palm wine? But surely the chief would not have mentioned drunkenness if there was no form of alcohol.

"Now we worship the one true God," Mary told Eme Ete after they had eaten.

She gathered the crewmen around her outside the yard and held a service. Many Okoyong women and men watched out of curiosity. Eme Ete remained, although Mary suspected she lived somewhere else. The more Mary spoke with the chief's sister the more she respected her. Eme Ete seemed to pick up on everything in an instant. It seemed Eme Ete was fascinated by the possibility that Mary might be able to remove some of the violence from their lives. Did Chief Edem feel that way, too? Had he allowed Mary to come because deep in his heart he hoped she would bring ways that were better than the Okoyong ways? She would pray again and again that was true.

"You will sleep in this hut with some of the chief's wives," said Eme Ete after several hours of talking.

Mary's "bed" was two layers of branches at right angles to each other covered by palm oil husks and leaves. The bed rustled from the movement of unseen vermin. Insects most certainly were there because they were everywhere. Perhaps a rat or two nestled in there too. Who knew for sure? Mary wasn't going to grope under the leaves to find out. The poor bed did not allow much sleep, but her heart was soaring. All night she praised God again for this glorious opportunity. How many times had she prayed to bring Jesus to the wilds? And God had at last generously answered her prayers.

"What is that?" cried Mary in the dawn light.

Noise had awakened her from that deep sleep that an exhausted person finally gets too close to dawn. Women were screaming. Men were shouting angrily. Dogs were snarling. Mary arose to peek out the hut. Her crewmen huddled nervously outside the yard.

The chief's sister Eme Ete finally arrived to explain what had happened. Her voice was so calm Mary suspected such commotion must happen often. Two women of the village had been shot at from the jungle, said Eme Ete. The women were unharmed, but their unseen assailants disappeared. This was typical of the Okoyong, shrugged Eme Ete. The jungle teemed with distrust. And no wonder. Violence lurked everywhere. A life could end in a heartbeat at any time. And it was not wild animals one had to fear most.

"Oh, how you people need the love of Jesus!" Mary told Eme Ete. The huge woman didn't appear to disagree.

Over the next days Mary explained her complete plan to Chief Edem. She wanted to open a mission in Ekenge. With help from other missionaries and the chief's people, she would build a church, a mission house, and a schoolhouse. She even made him promise that the mission house would be off-limits to his authority. Anyone who dwelled there had sanctuary.

He shrugged indifferently. How many refugees could this woman hide in a tiny hut?

Mary had this sanctuary in mind because she suspected many innocents were accused of witchcraft. If these Okoyong were like the old Efiks, they believed no one died young who had not been cursed by another.

To Chief Edem's obvious displeasure she journeyed two miles to Ifako just as she had said she would. There she found the chief sober. In fact he seemed very sensible. Was he ever drunk? Or did the chief of Ekenge lie to her? The chief of Ifako also agreed to her plan, even the sanctuary.

"Praise God," she murmured, "for two such villages only separated by a half-hour walk."

Mary and the crewmen departed. On the way back to Creek Town, the king's canoe was pelted for several hours by a storm, then halted by a tremendous tidal surge, resulting in another of those humorous ironies the natives could create. Mary wanted nothing more than delicious sleep inside her small curtained enclosure during the storm. But the crewmen kept loudly reprimanding each other to keep quiet so she could sleep. Only after the storm passed and they began busily rowing down the Calabar River again was she able to go to sleep—in spite of the coxswain's thumping drum.

Over the next weeks Mary steeled herself. Yes, she at long last had her entry into the wilds. But there were many trials ahead. These Okoyong in the wilds away from the rivers had no memory of British gunships, and indeed if they had ever heard such tales probably thought them clumsy lies to frighten them. The chiefs in the Okoyong were congenial enough—praise God—as long as she spoke of paradise and obediently slept in the yard with their wives. But what would happen the first time she raged against drunkenness? Against twin killing, if they practiced such an abomination? Against human sacrifice, if that was one of their vile customs? Against the deadly esere-bean test, if they allowed such a horror? More than one well-meaning Efik had approached her in Creek Town to tell her that her mission among the Okoyong was nothing short of suicide.

"If my death brings Christ to these people, I am willing," she told them.

She decided to take five of her bairns. There was dear Janie, of course, now six years old. Three boys included the Old Town chief's son Ekim, now eleven; Okin, a slave boy of eight; and a toddler of three. Almost constantly in Mary's arms was a baby girl. Her other children stayed in Creek Town, including the good-hearted girl, Inyang. Inyang was almost an adult, and Mary did not want her added to a pagan chief's harem. On the spur of the moment Mr. Bishop, the missionary printer, agreed to accompany Mary for the first days of the endeavor. Once again they traveled up the Calabar River in the king's canoe, departing Creek Town on late Saturday afternoon of August 4, 1888.

I am just four months shy of being forty years old, Mary realized with a start.

It was near nightfall when the canoe nudged the river bank where the path led inland to Ekenge. It seemed the dead of night within the dark jungle. It was raining, a normal occurrence for August. Mary loaded the two older boys with supplies for the march inland. Ekim balanced a box of bread, tea, and sugar on his head. Okin carried clanging pots. Janie and the three year-old supported each other. Mary lugged the baby and a bundle of supplies. Mr. Bishop was to follow her, leading crewmen with the rest of their supplies. Mary and her bairns trudged stubbornly through the wet jungle. She sang so the children would not be frightened. And perhaps a hungry leopard or two ran from her voice. With five children on a rainy night the four miles took an exhausting two hours. The huts at the chief's clearing were strangely quiet. She couldn't even see a fire.

"Is Ekenge deserted?" worried Mary.

She had heard natives often abandoned their villages because of curses and superstitions. But hadn't one of the Okoyong acted as if Ekenge had been there forever? Now, her first day and no one was there! She shouted. Two natives appeared out of the shadows and approached warily.

Mary had learned by now that a missionary had to be forceful at all times. "Where is everyone?" she demanded.

"We are slaves posted here for the night," they

informed Mary. "Nearly everyone else is at Ifako. The mother of their chief died."

"Lord have mercy on her soul," said Mary.

Mary praised God that Ekenge was not abandoned as she first thought. And she set about cooking a meal for the children in the yard and putting them to bed. Mr. Bishop still had not arrived, and she was getting very uneasy. Had the poor man encountered some beast on the way? Was he lost? Why hadn't she kept in contact with him? He was a printer, not an explorer. But she and the children had been moving so slowly she was sure the others were close behind.

Suddenly appearing in the fire's flickering light was Mr. Bishop. "Thank God you are here," cried Mary. But she realized he was alone. "Where are the others?"

"They would not come in the dark. They will come tomorrow."

"But tomorrow is the Lord's Day!"

Oh, Mr. Bishop, how could you? she thought. Little had she suspected her first serious confrontation in the wilds would not be with Chief Edem and his minions, but with King Eyo Honesty's crewmen! She couldn't believe she had to trudge back to the river in the dark. Four miles! But what choice did she have? After Mr. Bishop finished his hot meal, wearily she rose to go. Her boots sat by the fire, great clumps of mud. She hadn't had time to clean them. Well, she would not clean them this night. She headed back into the inky black jungle barefoot. It would be at least three hours to the river and back. Mr. Bishop was dismayed, but followed her, then even forged ahead to frighten off any curious beasts. Mary's feet became numb from striking tree roots.

Back at the river she awoke the sleeping crewmen, "Pick up the supplies and follow me."

"We are too tired," groaned one of the crewmen.

"Nonsense!" she snapped. "Pick up the supplies right now and follow me."

"But the jungle is full of dangers one cannot see in the dark," grumbled one of the more forthright crewmen. "Don't you know the night belongs to the beasts of the jungle? It is safer to walk in such places in the daylight."

"Trust God. The Almighty does not want you to work tomorrow on His day." Then she delivered the clincher, "I don't want to tell the king of your refusal to help me."

Grumbling, the crewmen picked up the remaining supplies and plodded off into the jungle behind Mary and Mr. Bishop. One and a half hours later they were all back in Ekenge. The crewmen seemed very relieved to find the village deserted. Any meeting with the Okoyong was fraught with danger. In the morning the crewmen were also relieved to find some of the villagers returning from the wake in Ifako either exhausted or intoxicated. Roosters were crowing as the "mourners" stumbled into their huts, not even inquiring about their visitors. The Okoyong of Ekenge would not be very belligerent this day. But Mary was not pleased. So the natives even in the wilds drank alcohol in great amounts, she fumed. Was it palm wine or some kind of native beer? It seemed unlikely they drank from stockpiles of rum and gin obtained in trade for their palm oil. In their fierce isolation they traded almost nothing as far as she knew. Oh, they had European guns, but those were obtained from people who traded with people who traded with people who traded with the Europeans on the coast.

"Come, Mr. Bishop, let us get ready for the services."

Mary and Mr. Bishop set up her table for the church service. On it was the Bible and the cross. The day was pure gloom. The sky that could be seen in the clearings for crops was overcast with steel-gray clouds. Her bruised feet were in agony. Fired by determination last night she had ignored the thumping her bare feet took on the trail. She couldn't ignore it now. It might be many days before she could even get her boots on. She sent boys through the village calling the natives to services. With Mr. Bishop and her older children she lifted her voice in hymns. Surely the people of Ekenge would flock to hear God's glory. But no. A mere handful of curious women stumbled up. They were red-eyed at that.

"Why all the noise?" they asked, frowning.

"This seems the saddest day of my life," Mary muttered.

Had her venture failed so quickly?

ELEVEN

It was many hours before most of the villagers of Ekenge, including Chief Edem, returned from the wake in Ifako. All day they straggled in, most sick from imbibing alcohol.

With little ceremony Mary and her children were installed in one of the chief's yards with six of his wives, several of their children, and his more fragile livestock. Mary's portion of the hut was small and filthy. But she could not work on the Lord's Day.

She held her fire until Monday morning. "Let's get to work, Mr. Bishop!"

With his help she went about changing her part of the hut. First, it was swept out. Then a hole was cut in one wall for a window she brought with her. With mud she filled in gaps in the poor fit. Holes in the walls were patched with mud too. A curtain was hung over the door. She did not bring her iron bed; she would sleep as the Okoyong did. The beds of branches and leaves on the floor were made anew. And she made it clear to all those who slept in the hut that the beds would be kept fresh and clean at all times. In the near future the hut would get a hard-mud floor, whitewashed if possible. This would do much to keep the vermin at bay. She also announced another fence would be raised within the yard to separate the hut from the livestock. The looks of the villagers of Ekenge carried little enthusiasm for her changes.

"Why bother?" their puzzled faces seem to say.

Mary stowed her belongings in her share of the hut, including boxes, books, a few pieces of furniture, a sewing machine, and a small organ. Her portion of the hut was so small, many of her belongings had to be lugged outside every night to make room for sleeping. Mary left a partition of boxes to separate her and the two girls from the three boys. Mary then said good-bye to Mr. Bishop and King Honesty Eyo's crewmen. The crewmen had never walked faster.

"The crewmen look like they just escaped death," observed Mary.

Over the next days a few of the Okoyong of Ekenge became enthusiastic for Mary's changes and her promise of better things in Christ. But the chief's sister Eme Ete warned Mary that if a native was too open in accepting the new things this carried great danger.

"Watch out for him." Eme Ete nodded at one young boy who eagerly helped.

The boy was especially bright and enthusiastic. Surely no one would harm such a treasure, reasoned Mary. So she was not too surprised to see the boy standing with the chief and his subchiefs near a pot of boiling palm oil one day. The boy had probably volunteered to help at some native custom. Many people had gathered to watch. She saw one man ladle up some boiling oil. The boy held out his arms.

"No!" screamed Mary.

Too late! Boiling oil seared the boy's arms and hands. The child lurched back as if shot, fell to the ground, and writhed in pain. Mary rushed to his aid. She hustled him into the yard. She treated this innocent victim of barbarism just as she had treated Okon's four wives at Ibaka. She cleaned his arms and hands, then gently applied an analgesic salve. She gave him an opiate and soothed him with reassuring words until the poor innocent fell asleep. She would keep him sedated for a day or two—until the worst part of the pain was over. Hopefully the child would not be scarred.

She next marched to the chief. "Why did you hurt a small boy?" she demanded to know.

"He is guilty of abandoning our sacred beliefs. His guilt was proven by the fact that the oil burned him. If he had been innocent the oil would not have harmed him. Everyone knows that."

Mary firmly told the chief that he could not go about punishing every villager who helped her. Otherwise, why had she come? Furthermore, there would be no more punishment for anything unless she personally was involved in their council.

He blinked, unbelieving. Hadn't she come to show them how to live better? Hadn't she come to doctor the sick with her fine medicines?

Mary bantered with him.

Seeming to take the chief's side was his sister Eme

Ete. But Mary soon realized the sister was actually helping her. Eme Ete was as clever a person as Mary had ever met. Eme Ete was able to advance an idea without seeming to do anything at all. No wonder she had admired the way Mary had used Chief Edem's jealousy of the chief of Ifako to get herself invited to live in Ekenge.

"I will allow you to sit in our councils," said the chief at last, scowling in disbelief at his own words.

It seemed to Mary that Chief Edem had consented only because of Eme Ete's shrewd maneuvering, plus his desire to use Mary's reputed skill with medicines. Perhaps it was insurance for his own health, even though he had little evidence yet that she could heal. At any rate the rumor of her skill with medicines must have been spreading throughout the wilds, because a crisis soon developed.

"We have a very dangerous situation here," warned Eme Ete as she summoned Mary from the yard.

On the way to Chief Edem's hut Eme Ete briefed Mary. Emissaries from a village many hours march away arrived to ask this new wonder doctor—the White Ma— to cure their sick Chief Krupka. Eme Ete's worry was that they would not be here unless the chief were gravely ill. And if he were gravely ill he would most likely die.

"Do you sacrifice people in the Okoyong when the chief dies?" asked Mary, dreading to hear the answer.

"Of course," said Eme Ete, blinking in wonder at Mary's ignorance. "Only a few months ago a chief died right near here. He was not even a great chief of a great clan, but it was only right that his four free wives join him. And let me see. . .yes, there were his slaves, too: eight men, eight women, and about twenty children, as I recall. . . ."

"Children, too? What evil!" Mary couldn't bring herself to add the numbers. "That many. . ."

"That wasn't the end of it, of course. The elders had to make sure the ones who bewitched the chief took the esere-bean test. . . ."

"Certain death," added Mary grimly. "Yes, I see I must go to this Chief Krupka and make sure he doesn't die."

Eme Ete shook her head at Mary's naiveté. She patiently explained that if Mary went to doctor the chief and he died, the result would be even worse. Mary might become a victim herself. Plus, the village of Ekenge would be held responsible, and the bloodshed would spread to Ekenge, as well! But when the two women spoke to Chief Edem, he could not voice any of these objections. Otherwise, it would sound as if he disagreed with their sacred customs or even that he feared the village of the sick chief. No, he found other reasons to object.

"The streams are too swollen," he protested. "A small woman like the White Ma would surely drown." He looked up the sky and added, "And it's still rainy."

"I put my trust in the Almighty," said Mary, looking up, too.

"We shall see," grunted Chief Edem in exasperation. "At least allow me to ask the emissaries to return to the village of Chief Krupka and come back with a larger escort."

Mary agreed. Was the chief merely delaying her departure, hoping that overnight she would change her mind? Or that Chief Krupka might die in the meantime? Perhaps. But the decision tormented her all night. Shouldn't she have prayed *before* she committed herself? It was just that she seemed presented with the opportunity to prevent another horrid case of human sacrifice, possibly involving dozens of lives. How could she refuse?

But the stakes were high. She prayed all night. Finally one of the warriors who guarded the women's compound told her the escort was waiting nearby on the jungle path. Mary said a cheerful good-bye to her children as if nothing unusual was happening, then trudged off in the rain toward the village many hours away. The decision still tormented her. Her five dear bairns were being left in jeopardy, too.

"God, surround them with your guardian angels," she prayed.

The journey was a watery hell. Streams were boiling red with mud-choked water, just as the chief said. Each crossing was a life-and-death challenge. Every brush with a leaf along the path seemed to drench her clothes. Every step seemed to plunge her feet into a slippery quagmire. Slowly she shed her European burdens: her mud-clumped boots that she wore less and less every day anyway; her sopping hat; even her umbrella, now as broken and misshapen as a crushed insect. Along the way Okoyong gathered to watch her pass. At first she thought they were contemptuous of such a bedraggled, barefoot creature as she, but it became evident that in their silent way they applauded her. Was the White Ma taking such risks for one of them? they wondered.

"Welcome to our village, White Ma," greeted an elder finally.

But the man's face was wooden with fear. The village with the sick Chief Krupka bristled with tension. Many expected to be murdered when he died. Many anticipated doing the murdering. The next days exhausted Mary. She barely remembered entering the chief's hut, determining he was sick from infection, sending runners to a distant medical facility to get a certain medicine, training women to nurse the chief after she was gone, and then leaving to trudge back to Ekenge.

She was not amazed at all that Chief Krupka was recovering and his village remained in peace. She had trusted God completely. But not so the villagers of Ekenge.

Eme Ete's mouth gaped. "You're alive!"

Mary smiled. "And so is their chief." Eme Ete should have smiled at that news but she did not. So Mary asked, "What is wrong?"

"Chief Edem is sick now. Come."

When Mary entered his hut she was aghast. By his bed a chicken flopped around a stake. Scattered on the floor were strange objects Mary knew were meant to be charms. Piled on the floor by the chief was inexplicable litter. The chief was on his stomach. His back was covered with charms too. But Mary could see the chief's back had a swollen area, obviously infected.

Chief Edem craned his neck to see who intruded. "You're alive, White Ma?" he gasped.

"So is their chief," she said, hoping to get that subject behind her.

"You saved him?" asked Chief Edem, hope now lifting his voice.

"What is all this nonsense lying on the floor beside you?" she asked.

"You don't know yet the heart of the Okoyong. I am cursed. The shaman has taken those evil things on the floor from my back."

Now she understood the pile of litter. Eggshells,

seeds, sticks, bones, teeth, feathers. All these accursed things, the shaman insisted, had been extracted from the chief's back.

"Nonsense," snorted Mary.

The chief was in turmoil. Should he believe Mary? Or his shaman? "The wicked people responsible for this treachery have already been arrested," he groaned. "They must be punished."

"That is only proper," said Eme Ete tactfully.

Mary humored him too while she treated his back. She cleaned the wound and disinfected it. And it was a good thing she hadn't argued, because after that visit the shaman refused to let her visit the chief again. Mary could do nothing now but pray she had done enough in one treatment for the chief's recovery. If he didn't recover, surely all the chief's wives would be made drunken, then strangled. And how many slaves? Around the village she saw men and women tied to posts. These were the ones deemed guilty of witchcraft by the elders. All these captives, observed Eme Ete, would be killed regardless of whether the chief recovered.

"No!" objected Mary.

But what could she do? She hadn't had time to instill anything but the tiniest Christian respect for life. She had hoped that Chief Edem would be so impressed by her success with the other sick chief—really the work of the Lord—that he would listen to her. But no. Winning Chief Edem's confidence was not going to be that easy. Others of the old ways had his ear. So she prayed without ceasing. She awoke New Year's Day of 1889, exhausted from praying.

"The chief still lives," Eme Ete informed her.

All the Okoyong lived with the constant threat of death, lamented Mary, and it was their own making. Even Eme Ete, so wise and serene, had barely escaped death once—by no more than the fluttering wings of a dying chicken. She had been the wife of a prominent chief in a nearby village. He had died and the elders decided to show great mercy by judging his free wives with the "chicken" trial. Each free wife brought the chicken of her choice to the elders. The elders were going to lop the head off each chicken and watch intently to see which way each one flopped and fluttered before expiring. One way meant innocence and life for the wife; the other way meant guilt and death. Eme Ete had fainted as her chicken was beheaded, but her very large presence proved her chicken fluttered the right way.

Her life with the chief when he was alive had not been safe, either. Her arms were scarred by bites he had inflicted on her in drunken rages.

"You poor dear," sympathized Mary.

In the next days, to the immense relief of everyone but the captives, Chief Edem recovered. Because of his recovery his wives and slaves would not be put to death, but the fate of the staked prisoners was still in doubt. Still, the chief's advisors kept Mary away from him.

So Mary appealed for mercy in the strongest of terms to Eme Ete. With every bit of logic she could summon, she implored her friend to convince the chief that a truly great man showed mercy. Chief Edem's mercy would show everyone he did not fear these men and women.

Eme Ete liked that logic very much. "Yes, my brother might like that. His heart is not black like the hearts of some of the other chiefs."

It was the chief's son who days later brought Mary the chief's decision. Chief Edem must surely be the most merciful chief in all of Okoyong, insisted the son. He had already released every prisoner—except a mere slave woman, who was not even given the esere-bean test that she deserved but sold to traders.

By now Mary knew this story about the slave woman was not true. In fact she had been secretly murdered. But to protest would be to betray Mary's informant. That would trigger more killing. So contrary to how she really felt, she acted pleased at the chief's "mercy."

Drumbeats suddenly erupted. The son's face lit up. "That is the signal that the celebration must begin for my father's recovery."

Much to Mary's disgust a wild binge of drinking started. By now she realized that the Okoyong did drink rum and gin as well as a palm wine. They drank so steadily she hadn't been aware of the universal drinking. Like some Europeans many had developed an apparent immunity to its effects. They showed no sign of intoxication. Only during the wildest drinking bouts was it apparent. But Mary now suspected drinking was epidemic among the adults. She had heard children were encouraged to drink to entertain the bored adults with their drunken antics.

"Barbarism takes all forms," she told her own bairns, "and getting a child drunk is a very evil form."

In the midst of superstition and turmoil she began her schools. The natives would never be self-sufficient in the gospel until they could read and write. She had many years of experience at teaching, so she knew it took very little to get started. She walked to a clearing in Ifako in the afternoon and gathered her young pupils, who sat on logs and listened as she drilled them with alphabet cards. They learned symbols for numbers too and began to add and subtract. She ended every session with raucous singing of the exercises, then a scripture lesson, and finally a prayer to the true God.

She held a similar school in Ekenge in the evening. This evening gathering drew adults, too, of which a handful seemed fired by the power of these new symbols. But most of the adults stopped coming after the novelty wore off.

Violent crises seemed never to end. When one crisis was resolved, another appeared. Chiefs from other villages visited often and became drunk and belligerent. Every dispute seemed now to call for Mary to intercede. Was it shrewd Eme Ete who prompted Chief Edem to call for her intercession?

Often Mary was up all night scurrying this way and that way on jungle paths, heading off bands of drunken warriors with murder in their hearts.

Often a dispute would be settled only to erupt again if someone found some object planted in their path to put a curse on them. Always Mary tried to snatch up these items and demonstrate utter contempt for such nonsense.

"This is nothing but the root of a plantain!" she would shout in scorn.

To ease Mary's fatigue, Eme Ete helped her more and more in the yard. Usually now Eme Ete cooked the meals for her. She did far more than that. Eme Ete was Mary's source of all impending acts by Chief Edem and his elders. Soon the chief and the elders began to regard

Mary as uncanny in her ability to sense trouble and head it off. Mary's influence grew ever greater. But it was Eme Ete behind much of her magic. And it was Eme Ete who hinted to Mary that she needed to leave the yard.

"But how?" puzzled Mary.

Then she remembered the words of Livingstone. Once on friendly terms with a chief, a missionary must not ask the chief for permission to do something. Just go ahead and do it. So Mary took the children and cleared an area in the brush where she wanted her own mission house.

If asked by a curious villager, Mary shrugged. "Chief Edem promised me a mission house."

Many villagers could not resist helping. "Let me show you how to make a nice wall, White Ma," one would say. Then he would beat stalks of bamboo until they were soft, then interlace them into a neat panel.

Such a panel was attached to well-anchored posts, then daubed with red mud. These mud walls soon formed Mary's immaculate two-room house about twelve feet to a side with a spacious verandah. The roof was a thatch of palm leaves. The floor was hardened mud.

The house became more and more elaborate. With mud Mary made a fireplace, flanked by hutches with niches for dishes. She even made a "sofa" of mud. It was surprisingly comfortable—when compared to lying on a bed of sticks. The next step was to smoke the interior of the house for many hours to dry out the materials and to drive out all the vermin. Then before moving in her furnishings she had brought from Creek Town, the walls were whitewashed inside and outside. She would add large sheds on each side of the house later. All she needed was a carpenter to make proper windows and a door.

Still, most of the Okoyong acknowledged in wonder that it was the finest residence in Ekenge.

Mary surprised them even further. "This is only temporary. The real mission house will be nicer."

Their jaws dropped. How could that be? Mary planned on a two-story house, not that she knew how to do it herself. But a carpenter would know how. She also planned on cultivating in her own garden every kind of plant that might grow in Okoyong, besides the manioc, plantains, corn, cocoyams, and yams already grown there.

"My chief wants you," a grim-faced warrior from Ifako told Mary one day.

TWELVE

Have I alienated the chief of Ifako by honoring Ekenge with such a nice mission house? Mary wondered. *And what will he do to me?*

When she arrived in Ifako she found once again she had benefited from the rivalry between the two villages. Apparently after the chief in Ifako heard of Mary's mission house in Ekenge he wanted to make sure Ifako got the church. The villagers of Ifako had cleared a parcel of land for a church. Not only had they done that, but they piled stacks of bamboo, palm leaves, and other building materials. They were ready to begin building a church twenty-five feet wide and thirty feet long! Mary couldn't believe how great was God's blessing on her these days. And she noticed the Okoyong who helped her build the church did not drink alcohol. A few admitted to her in wonder that they couldn't remember not drinking every day of their lives. So she concluded it was boredom that drove many of them to drink.

She stored that useful information in her mind. *Somehow I must promote industry someday,* she noted.

But first she had to see her new buildings finished. The church was formally opened. For that occasion, Mary delved into mission boxes full of clothing she had been accumulating. The Okoyong children were soon all decked out in colorful European clothing. The women were envious, and Mary promised to clothe them, too, as soon as possible. To excite them even more she said they could create their own dresses with her sewing machine. With the chiefs gathered for the opening, Mary once again made them assure her that the church building was her sacred ground and that no one could enter it and take away a refugee.

"At last a mission house in Ekenge and a church in Ifako," she gushed to Eme Ete. "We lack only a schoolhouse, but we can use the church for that in the meantime. And, oh yes, we must have proper windows and doors. Well, I'm sure God will provide all that very soon. . . ."

"Hello there, lass!" yelled a man's voice one day in the summer of 1889.

Mary was sitting in her new yard amid children, goats, and chickens. This young Scotsman named Charles Ovens was a most welcome visitor. He was a carpenter, sent to Calabar by the Foreign Mission Board. The local committee sent him on to Ekenge. Fresh to the tropics, he was bursting with energy and good cheer. He didn't know the native languages yet, but over the weeks he influenced many a native with his singing. As he sawed and planed and hammered, he sang old Scottish songs so plaintive, so melancholy, that they transcended language.

"His songs make my heart ache and my eyes water, Ma," one of the Okoyong explained to Mary.

What a contrast Charles Ovens was to most of the missionaries, so worn down and bedraggled from heat, disease, and never ending crises. Mary was the ultimate example of unremitting stress on a missionary. She had not been in Ekenge and Ifako one year yet, and she could scarcely believe she had freed so many people about to be sacrificed, resolved so many arguments about to erupt in bloodshed, and escaped so many brushes with death herself. It all seemed nothing less than a repetition of her hero Livingstone's life, so perilous—yes, so miraculous. It surely meant she, too, worked through the Holy Spirit. And it was while Charles Ovens was putting in windows and doors that another crisis developed.

"Ma, come quick!" screamed an Okoyong.

Mary rushed off. A young man had been felling a tree to build a house for his bride-to-be. He misjudged its fall and was struck down. He was unconscious, seriously injured. When Mary saw that the young man was Etim, she knew the situation was explosive. If Etim did not recover, Chief Edem and the elders would deem his death the result of witchcraft. Revenge would be exacted. Chaos and barbarism would reign once again. Many would die to set things "right" again. For Etim was a subchief so important he was regarded by many a chief.

"And even more," murmured Mary as she doctored him, "Etim is the son of Chief Edem."

Every day for two weeks Etim weakened. Mary sent word to Duke Town that she might need help. The missionaries there now knew that Mary had confirmed that the Okoyong sacrificed humans for chiefs. What they—or she—could do to prevent such a slaughter though, she did not yet know. Finally one morning, as the end for young Etim approached, she surprised several Okoyong in the hut, including the young man's uncle Ekpenyong, trying last desperate measures to get some response out of him. They blew smoke in his nose, rubbed pepper into his eyes, and screamed into his ears. By the time Mary shooed them away Etim was dead.

"Someone must die for the curse that killed our great Etim!" the men shouted as they rushed off to inform Chief Edem.

Chief Edem and his elders held a council and decided the nearby small village of Chief Akpo was surely responsible for the foul deed. Etim had relatives there and who was more likely to carry a grudge—fermented from envy of Etim's achievements—than a relative? Warriors from Ekenge stormed off to that village, captured a few stragglers, and burned the huts. The prisoners, both men and women, were brought back to Ekenge and tied to stakes. Soon they would be given a potion with the esere bean to test their guilt or innocence. Of course, hinted shrewd Eme Ete to Mary, a grand funeral for the young man might greatly delay acts of revenge.

"Yes," agreed Mary, "it wouldn't be right for the bereaved to ignore elaborate preparations to honor Etim."

So Mary searched her boxes of donated clothing before preparing Etim. What better model for finery than King Eyo Honesty? Soon Etim was dressed in a smart European suit and festooned in bright silks. On his head was a top hat trimmed with brilliant parrot feathers. Mary and her helpers then lugged Etim into a clearing and tied him in a chair under an umbrella. In his hands Mary inserted a whip and a silver-topped walking stick, symbols of great power. Tucked under his arms was a mirror in which he would behold his own grandeur in the beyond. On a table next to Etim his aunt Eme Ete displayed his war trophies, including skulls of some of his victims. The Okoyong of Ekenge gathered around.

"Never have we seen any chief receive such honor!" prompted Eme Ete.

"Etim is magnificent!" agreed the gawking Okoyong.

"We must celebrate this unmatched event!" commanded Chief Edem, staggered by his son's magnificence. "Bring out the spirits."

Now it was Mary who couldn't believe her eyes. Case after case of gin were brought into the clearing. Kegs of rum appeared. The Okoyong quickly began to deplete the chief's supply of spirits. They danced and sang and shouted. This was a great event in their lives.

Meanwhile Mary and Charles Ovens kept their eyes on the prisoners. No drunks—many of the dancers brandished guns and machetes—could be allowed to suddenly murder one of the poor captives.

Yes, worried Mary, she had created a delay. But how would she free the prisoners? She even saw a few of the more sober Okoyong—those who preferred killing to drinking—pounding the esere beans into the toxic powder on a great pounding stone.

She prayed all during the drunken frenzy. *God, please provide an answer for this dilemma!* And at last the answer came to her.

She went directly to Chief Edem. "You may not try the prisoners with the esere bean!"

"What nonsense!" he screamed.

"Raise Etim from the dead!" shouted one of the elders. "Then we will free your precious prisoners."

Mary dragged her chair in front of the captives as if to barricade any attempt on them. This seemed to ignite the revelers. They began to threaten her, curse her. All this time she armored herself with prayer.

Her prayer life since coming to Ekenge had become intense anyway. Many times she was sure she had passed beyond hope to utter trust in God answering her prayers. Yes, prayer was mountainous in her life. Had there ever been a day she had not talked to God? An hour?

And she was no Pollyanna about it. Often she had been disappointed in her prayer life. In her earliest years she had read of great mystics and tried with all her power to meditate as they had. But her mind always wandered. That had depressed her until she got older and realized meditation wasn't intended for her.

And what of those countless hours she prayed that her father would not return home drunk? Her prayers were never answered, she thought. She felt rejected by God. Perhaps that was why Scottish men rattled her so; they reminded her not only that God had rejected her but that she had doubted God. Of course now she knew God had not rejected her. Her father had exercised his free will—a priceless gift from God—and he had failed himself and his family miserably. Oh, how he had failed. But prayer had never failed Mary for her own needs. Always short of food, short of money, short of clothing, short of help, always she prayed.

"And how You provide for me, God!" she sang in praise.

Yes, she routinely prayed all though the day. And she urged others to do the same. "Money is nice but say a prayer for the work," she urged people who wanted to help. In fact this very moment in this most desperate situation in Ekenge she did not doubt there were friends in Calabar, in Scotland, in England, who were praying for her safety and for peace in Okoyong. She was certain of that. But most important she was sure God would respond—if it was His will. If it was not His will then why should she be disappointed?

"I am nothing," she prayed. "Do Your will, God."

Finally one shaman stepped forward as if to say "Enough of this nonsense; unchain the prisoners and let's get started." Mary rose from her chair to protest, and he shoved her aside. After all the prisoners were unchained, he held out the cup with the esere-bean potion to a woman captive. She obediently took the cup. Mary stepped forward and took the woman's other hand as if to comfort her. The shaman eyed Mary suspiciously, his own hand half-raised as if to strike Mary down.

"*Ifehe!*" screamed Mary and yanked the woman toward the jungle.

Charles Ovens and all the other prisoners scrambled after them. Mary glanced back. Where were their pursuers? The men of Ekenge had drunk too much to think quickly. They had drunk too much to catch them. But the dash into the jungle was only a diversion because Mary quickly worked her way back to the mission house. Chief Edem had long ago promised that it would be off-limits to his authority. To her continued amazement every one of the doomed captives arrived inside her yard safely. Charles Ovens, too. But it wasn't long before the chief and his warriors appeared. They were red-eyed drunks, suddenly sober.

Chief Edem shouted, "In my great mercy, I have thought of a compromise. I will allow all but three to go free." He named the three. "How much more generous can I be? But those three must drink the esere bean. Two are related to Etim. Surely they must be responsible. And the third is related to Akpo, chief of the offending village." Chief Edem shouted his conclusion even louder, "I have made more concessions for the White Ma than for anyone before. Now let me have the three prisoners!"

"No," said Mary, standing in front of the mission house, arms folded in defiance.

During the standoff, visitors from other villages began to appear. This ruckus in Ekenge was quite an event. Disturbing rumors reached Mary. Egbo runners were coming. Egbo "justice" among the Okoyong? Did the various tribes have so many customs in common? Rumors swirled that Chief Edem wasn't getting justice done. Perhaps he was weak in his grief. Perhaps he could no longer rule. This made Chief Edem even angrier.

"I made a mistake giving you sanctuary here," he said. "We will have to burn this mission house down!"

Eme Ete now stepped forward. "Perhaps Chief Edem would be so merciful as to try just one prisoner."

"One?" mumbled Chief Edem in disappointment. Before Mary could object he quickly seized the chance. "Yes, I agree to that. There is one woman prisoner so vile I can accept her trial as full payment for the death of my son."

Mary was in agony. She didn't want even one innocent to die. But perhaps Eme Ete was right. Perhaps she could detect in her brother that he was seconds away from ordering wholesale murder—not only the prisoners but the two missionaries, too. Mary found herself arguing weakly for this last prisoner's life. After all, it seemed she had been awake for ages. She was worn out.

"Miss Slessor! Mr. Ovens!" called voices from the jungle.

Two missionaries from Duke Town approached the yard of the mission house. "Do you see, Chief Edem, how greatly we honor your son?" cried Mary. "We have summoned men all the way from the distant seashore to attend your son, to prepare him for the beyond. Let us not do anything hasty."

The body of Etim was now placed in a fine wooden coffin crafted hurriedly by Charles Ovens. Then the two newcomers went through a solemn ritual with Etim, committing his soul to the hereafter. Then they set up a lantern slide show. The show told of modern European wonders and then the greatest story of all: the God made man and his sacrifice for all human sin. This colorful show seemed to pacify the villagers. But after Etim's burial a fight broke out among some drunken mourners. Once again in a heartbeat a man died. The victor cut off his fallen victim's head and carried it proudly back to his hut.

"Don't worry," Eme Ete comforted Mary. "It's nothing. Just an old quarrel."

But Mary never stopped praying. God must change Chief Edem's heart. She knew the crisis over Etim was not over. And at long last the Egbo runners stormed into the village masked in garish colors, lashing out with whips, demanding justice.

But Chief Edem stopped them. He was haggard but very sober now. More, he seemed changed. "Go away," he told the runners. He had already administered justice to those responsible for his son's death. He nodded toward the woman chained in front of the mission house. The runners in their garish masks paused. Mary knew they were studying the chief. Should they press him?

"We have received false stories," shouted one. "We see now the chief in his wisdom has dealt out justice."

The runners slunk off into the jungle, their whips dragging listlessly. Now Mary knew the real status of Egbo "justice" among the Okoyong. Although the Egbos tried to extend their influence into the wilds, the Okoyong had little use for them. The Egbos could not stand up to a strong chief. Mary was tense as Chief Edem posted guards by the woman but soon the crowd evaporated. Mary thanked the two missionaries from Duke Town and told them the long convoluted story before they too departed.

Days later Chief Edem announced that on much reflection he decided Chief Akpo was the only one who could atone for his son's death. But until Akpo could be captured the woman captive would be held in chains.

Still, news spread that the White Ma had done the impossible. She had for the first time in Okoyong prevented human sacrifice for the death of a chief. To make sure this became reality Mary argued for forgiveness every time she saw Chief Edem.

"Show mercy to Chief Akpo," she pleaded.

But Chief Edem would not agree.

"He seems to be struggling with the devil," Mary told Charles Ovens.

The crisis seemed not over but smoldering. Rumors were floating about that Chief Edem's brother Ekpenyong had something to do with Etim's death. One day people rushed to Mary and urged her to come to Ekpenyong's clearing. He was out of his mind, demanding to take the esere-bean test! When Mary arrived she saw Ekpenyong was drunk. His wives were trying to take a bag away from him. Mary, certain the bag contained the poison beans, managed to snatch it away herself. Forty of the deadly beans were in the bag. She stalled Ekpenyong until Chief Edem himself intervened, ordering his brother not to take the test.

Even then, the aftermath of Etim's death was not over. The murder and beheading after the burial of Etim had not been avenged. Feelings built that the victim was an innocent, murdered by a particularly nasty older son in a particularly nasty clan. Skirmishes began.

Once again, Mary had to intervene. "Couldn't the warring factions let a chief from a distant village arbitrate?" she suggested.

Amazingly, they agreed. Mary began to suspect most people—even the chiefs—in the Okoyong despised their murderous ways, but no one knew how to stop them.

Eme Ete came to Mary later to tell her what happened. Blood for blood was the distant chief's verdict: The murderer must die. The guilty man asked that slaves be substituted for his death; that was often permitted.

147

No, said the distant chief, that compensation was not just. Then to Mary's horror, Eme Ete revealed that the distant chief agreed to let the guilty man substitute his younger brother!

"But the younger brother escaped," confided Eme Ete.

"Praise God for that," answered Mary. But later she was sickened to learn the youth had been captured and hanged.

In all the deadly turmoil Mary's own household of bairns grew. One newcomer seemed miraculous. It only reinforced Mary's reputation as a miracle worker. Natives spoke of a baby abandoned on a certain path. It was not clear if the baby was a twin or not, but the mother was dead. Mary rushed to get it. Praise God, the baby girl had not been found by a leopard. But the child had been severely damaged by insects. Portions of her nose and lips had been eaten away. Mary nursed the tiny thing back to health. Meanwhile, Eme Ete spread the word far and wide that the child was not a twin. Removed of that stigma, the girl was now regarded as a "wonder child." She became known as "Little Mary."

In all the turmoil the missionary work had to be done too. Charles Ovens not only added windows and doors to all the buildings but had constructed a second story on the mission house. Mary and the others built another two rooms onto the church to serve as a rectory. The results were so pleasing Mary led all the villagers in tours of the mission house and the church.

"What is that?" asked visitors all day long.

Mary answered, "A sewing machine for making fine clothes," or, "An organ for playing wonderful music," or,

"A clock for showing the exact time of day or night," or, "A dress of muslin," or, "A book with words written in symbols," or a hundred other responses.

Yes, she was proud of her examples of civilization, and she had the most excellent reason for showing them off. She wanted to create a desire in the natives to acquire some of the civilized objects themselves. Once, she had been contemptuous of the desire of Efiks to acquire "iron pots and shiny English plates." But she had been wrong. Now she knew the Okoyong needed an incentive to work, to be industrious.

She had tried to get traders from Calabar to visit Okoyong and they refused. The reputation of the Okoyong was too frightening. Besides, the traders at Calabar knew what it had taken Mary months to learn: The chiefs had warriors in hidden posts along all the jungle paths. If a traveler had the sanction of a chief, he passed without harm; if not, death!

"Somehow we must go ahead and push trade into Okoyong," Mary told Charles Ovens. "Let us pray for guidance."

Then she had an idea so preposterous it was no wonder she had never thought of it before.

THIRTEEN

I will have the chiefs of Okoyong go to the traders at Calabar!" Mary told an amazed Charles Ovens.

Why not try it? She wrote King Eyo Honesty and appealed to him: Could he send the chiefs of Okoyong an invitation to Creek Town? The king did just that. After his invitation arrived though, the Okoyong chiefs refused to go. Mary pleaded with them. The chiefs told her she might as well have been asking them to step off the edge of the earth! And they must go unarmed? What self-respecting Okoyong would walk about with no spear, no dagger, no machete, no gun! And what did these chiefs of Okoyong have to trade with the traders of Calabar?

"Palm oil, plantains, manioc," insisted Mary.

It was Chief Edem's acquiescence—swayed behind the scenes by his very clever sister—that broke down the resistance. Soon several canoes full of chiefs, warriors, trade goods, and one small, redheaded missionary headed down the Calabar River. At one point the sharp-eyed Mary spotted the glint of metal under a sack of manioc flour.

"It is so hard being righteous," prayed Mary. "God, protect me."

She seized the razored machetes and hurled them into the river. They twisted and swirled into the depths like silvery fish. The chiefs pretended not to notice. Otherwise, they would be forced to do something terrible to this extremely troublesome woman.

"Creek Town ahead!" yelled someone in the lead canoe.

Creek Town astonished the chiefs of Okoyong. King Eyo Honesty and the Efiks had wealth they had never dreamed of. Yes, they had been amazed to see the White Ma's possessions in Ekenge and Ifako. But King Eyo Honesty's possessions dazzled them. What riches. Why, his famous brass cannon on his canoe was a mere trifle compared to his other riches.

The opening banquet in the king's large hall set the tone. The Okoyong chiefs gaped around as they were seated on one side of the immense banquet table. On the other side of the table sat Mary with other white missionaries. Sitting at the head of the table of course was King Eyo Honesty VII, wearing a shiny black top hat adorned with parrot feathers. He held a scepter of the finest polished silver.

The king clapped his hands, fingers ringed with huge red and blue and green stones. Several women entered the great hall. They attended Mary first, a wise thing ordered by the king. That way the guests from Okoyong would learn what was expected. Mary made a great show of extending her hands over the basin a woman offered her. The woman poured water over her hands, and another woman dabbed her hands dry with a towel. After every guest had hands washed and dried, women entered, bringing large silver platters and bowls covered with cloths. The king clapped his hands again. The bounty was uncovered.

"So much!" gasped one of the chiefs from Okoyong.

Yams stuffed with peppers. Black soup. Fufu. Manioc and fish soup. Fried plantains. Cocoyams. Bananas. Corn. Roast goat. Chicken. Beef. Fish. Sweets. Even Mary was surprised. The king's famous table improved with every occasion. The Okoyong chiefs ate much of the food tentatively, betraying ignorance of such food. But soon they relaxed. The king took the opportunity to advance the gospel. Following the banquet was a church service. After that the king took the chiefs down to the river to show them an armored warship of the British navy.

"It is like a porcupine all bristling with guns," one Okoyong chief gasped, "but as big as a mountain!"

The king explained to them that the chiefs along the coast had agreed to be protected by the British. The entire land was called the "Niger Coast Protectorate." So far, the king explained, the British were content to merely see that the trade in palm oil was not disrupted in any way. But the day was soon coming when the British would send armed soldiers into the jungle to arrest people who practiced the terrible old ways of twin murder and human sacrifice.

Even Mary was surprised by this assertion. But she seized the opportunity. "The gospel will teach you the right way to behave," she told the puzzled Okoyong chiefs.

Then the chiefs were taken to a market where they traded their goods. They acquired fine cutlery, dishes, elegant fabrics, top hats, walking sticks, and enough trinkets to please everyone back in Okoyong. Mary suspected the king had ordered the merchants to offer more than generous terms to the visitors. No rum or gin were allowed to be traded, but the Okoyong chiefs were clearly smitten by what the coast traders had to offer. Could they indeed trade their simple jungle produce for such finery? It seemed the answer was yes.

So the chiefs returned to Okoyong burning with ambition to acquire more of these goods. Why couldn't they live as well as King Eyo Honesty and rule as nobly too? The transformation had started.

Chief Edem seemed shaken. With no ceremony the woman prisoner was released.

Mary rushed to Chief Edem. "Does this mean you have shown great mercy to Akpo?"

"My heart has no vengeance in it for Akpo," he admitted. "Let him return to his village."

Forgiveness? From a chief in Okoyong? Mary blinked in disbelief. "You are generous, Chief Edem."

"I am weary of our old ways," he said. "I have seen how King Eyo Honesty lives. I have seen how a great chief behaves. I intend to help Akpo rebuild his village."

Mary was astonished. How great was the power of Christ! Because it could be nothing else that changed the chief's heart from harboring evil superstition to harboring the love and forgiveness of the gospel. She reflected on how once she had only half-believed the story of Daniel in the lions' den. But now she knew. She had faced worse. And God was merciful to her. Oh, how merciful.

But something else wonderful had happened at Creek Town during the visit of the chiefs. Mary had met a Scotsman, Charles Morrison. He was a teacher at the mission in Duke Town. He sought her out. He seemed in awe of her. Yet he was articulate and well-read, causing her to dredge up fond memories of her young reading days. Moreover he was from Kirkintilloch, a village near Glasgow but also near Blantyre, Livingstone's roots. His attentions began to appear almost like courtship.

Mary was startled. Surely she was imagining it. Her liking for him flamed up inside her. Yes, she liked him very much. She had to admit it. She wasn't going to lie to herself. So in a private moment she asked him outright just what his interest in her was.

He was blunt, too. He proposed marriage. All through her sputtered protests he calmly explained how much he loved her and how he wished to come to Ekenge as her coworker—and husband. Mary experienced intense emotion, but was it love?

Now back in Ekenge her heart ached over this Charles Morrison. She felt as if she carried the weight of the world on her shoulders. Yet Christ said his burden was light. Did that mean her affection for Charles Morrison was wrong? For the truth was that he was only twenty-five. Past forty, Mary felt like a much older sister to him. He was so young. Besides, she had long ago put aside thoughts of a husband. She had married Christ. And an ideal marriage it was. Still, the young man was very nice, very polite, very forward in his affection for her. Should she resent his affection? Good grief, she scolded herself, how could she face death against Okoyong warriors one moment and act like a foolish coquette the next?

She resolved to forget her young suitor. *Thank you, Charles Morrison, for flattering a weathered old jungle lass,* she told herself, remembering his eager young face, *but she's almost worn out.*

Charles Ovens reminded her one day just how frazzled she was. He arrived from Duke Town just as she was preparing to conduct the church service for the Lord's Day. He carried his huge tool kit, looking bewildered. He had come to put the finishing touches on the second floor of the mission house.

Mary gave him a withering look. "What can you be thinking, Charles Ovens, traveling for your work on the Lord's Day?"

Charles burst her bubble gently. "Miss Mary Slessor, today is Monday."

"Monday!" She locked her eyes on him. "And I was whitewashing walls yesterday on the Lord's Day! Well, for the natives' peace of mind, we'll just have to pretend today is the Lord's Day. Get ready for the service."

"But I already observed it yesterday. . . ." Then noting the steel in Mary's eyes, he quietly set down his tool kit and took a seat on a bench. But after the service he was direct. "Mary, you are run-down. You need a furlough."

"It will pass. I just have a lot on my mind."

But it was not her mind. Perhaps because she was already run-down, Mary succumbed to a severe attack of jungle fever.

Charles Morrison came to Ekenge and nursed her for a while. Feelings of affection flamed for him again.

Ovens then took it upon himself to contact the mission committee in Duke Town and request a furlough for Mary. By the time she felt better, her replacement, Miss Dunlop, had already been notified.

Mary shrugged. Her desire to return to England or Scotland had died with her family. But could she stand as an exception? Who wanted to leave the work they loved in Africa and go off to give speeches? Would every hard-driven, broken-down missionary say in the future, "Well, Mary Slessor never took a furlough"? So she packed her belongings. Of course Janie, now eight years old, would go with her.

Her trek to the canoe on the Calabar River was interrupted. "You must come quick," begged a messenger from a distant village. "One of our freemen has been hurt."

"I'll give you medicine to take back," she said wearily.

But then came another messenger with news the freeman had died. In a heartbeat the situation became armed conflict. Now one clan would battle another. After all, no young man died accidentally. Surely he must have died from a curse. Against all advice of those in Ekenge, Mary trudged off to the village with the messengers. Although she traveled for many hours the path seemed familiar. Then in the darkness all familiarity evaporated. Finally her guides stopped. It was the distant village. But no one there wanted to show her where any of the chiefs were located.

"There is no war here," insisted frightened villagers.

"You may fool a woman," snapped Mary, "but you can't fool her God!"

She persisted. Finally she found one chief's clearing. The chief refused to see her.

"What is she doing here?" demanded his warriors. Then one of the elders came to say there would be no fighting until Mary had heard everyone's side of the story. In the meantime she should relax. Women would make her comfortable. The elder left with the warriors.

"Run after them, White Ma!" screamed one of the women.

Soothing her fears had been a ruse. The chief and his warriors had already slipped away on the warpath. Mary ran after them. She could barely see in the dawn light. But at last she stumbled upon them, crouching outside the other clan's clearing, readying for an attack.

"What a cheap trick!" she shouted. "Behave like men, not young brats!" One man stood up and approached. Mary was stunned. "Chief Krupka!"

"Yes, White Ma, it is I whom you nursed back to life."

"What is the meaning of all this?"

He whispered to her sadly, "Why are we all responsible for one of our men's misdeeds? It was one of our warriors who wounded the freeman who died. Our warrior was drunk, but it was no accident. Still, we must defend ourselves against revenge, mustn't we? So we will strike first." His voice conveyed the insanity of the situation.

Mary wanted to rush right over to the other clan and open negotiations. But she knew it was best to act calm. "I will help you settle it. But I'm going to eat now." She forced a yawn. "In the meantime pick two of your most prudent men to represent your side in a palaver."

Eventually Mary arranged the palaver with two men

representing each side. She told all those assembled they were on the brink of a new age for the Okoyong. These men could become legends, great heroes wise enough to think of substituting arbitration for war. No war? This caused the clan who had lost their man to grumble. And several times warriors from both sides ventured up to the palaver, shaking their fists and threatening. Mary had to get up each time and run them off.

"*Soi! Wara du!*" she shouted at them, as if they were pesky children. It meant, "Shoo! Go away!"

And the warriors did back off each time. She was exhausted. How many hours had she been awake? But she had to persist. What was her exhaustion compared to human lives? Finally the four men arbitrated a settlement. The guilty clan agreed to pay the other clan. The amount was so enormous Mary was stunned.

This really told her that the Okoyong did not want to kill each other. They just had never had a mechanism other than "blood for blood" for settling disputes, before Mary showed them how. Despite her fatigue, she felt wonderful.

As she departed one of the younger warriors asked, "As long as we are here, White Ma, can't we have a small fight?"

"No!" groaned Mary, restraining herself from swatting the numskull over the head with her umbrella.

She wearily marched back to Ekenge, reflecting that a missionary could never relax for long in the Okoyong. Not pausing to rest, she took a canoe down the Calabar River. She must not miss her steamer to England.

There was barely time to see Charles Morrison before she boarded the steamer at Duke Town.

He appealed to her, "Won't you ask the Foreign Mission Board back in Scotland if we can work together at Ekenge as man and wife?"

To her astonishment, she agreed!

Back in England by January 1891 Mary first visited the graves of her mother and sister Jane in Topsham. She thanked those there who had made their last days comfortable. Then she was off to Scotland for the inevitable speaking engagements. As reluctant as she was to speak, she knew it had to be done, and it had to be done as cheerfully as possible. Moreover, she was more sure than ever of what she wanted to say.

"We need dedicated, affectionate women missionaries who are not afraid to work," she said. "After all, whitewashing a wall or patching a roof is almost as important as teaching a child to read or conducting a church service. And we want women who can tend a baby or teach a child to wash his hands and face—as well as teach him to read and write. We want women with tact who can smooth things over or even cheerfully ignore a snub if they have to. These women must be willing to work anywhere, do any job for Christ. Smile and persevere. In the wilds like Okoyong we must teach the first principles of everything!" Of course she urged one and all to send whatever they could to Okoyong. Castoff clothing was a great blessing to people who had nothing.

Her accomplishments among the Okoyong, perhaps the most savage people on earth, were heralded in the *Missionary Record* of the church. Mary, who had avidly read the magazine with her mother, could scarcely believe she was featured. Mission officials begged her to write articles herself.

"The record of this majestic work must be preserved," insisted the mission board.

She made another splash in the *Missionary Record*, too. She was struck by the prevailing opinion that Africans were too backward to learn trades. She couldn't ignore such an ignorant attitude. So she crafted a long, reasoned letter to the *Missionary Record* refuting this belief with facts. "Please, come to Calabar," she urged, "and teach the Africans trades!" She prayed that the letter would have some effect. Later she heard the mission board was stirred by this plea.

But the board was not receptive to her request that she and Charles Morrison work together at Ekenge—bonded in marriage. Just how serious was she? Some of them detected a lack of enthusiasm on Mary's part. They tested her by putting obstacles in her way: Charles Morrison was a teacher; he was needed at Duke Town—was Mary willing to return to Duke Town?

Heavens no, she protested. In fact she felt an anger rising in her that was wrath. And in her heart she knew her desire for marriage was not strong enough. Perhaps Charles Morrison was deeply in love with her, but she had to admit that she preferred life in Okoyong without Charles to life in Duke Town with Charles. So in effect, she made her choice. The more she reflected on their hasty plans the more unreal they seemed. Slowly she realized she had made the board make a decision that she was too smitten by a man's attention to make herself. Because once the decision was made she felt no pain.

All I feel is relief, she admitted to herself.

By February 1892 she was ready to return to Africa. She was something of a celebrity among the church people. But she would return to Okoyong even more than an extraordinary missionary. In 1891 Sir Claude MacDonald had been appointed the consul of the Niger Coast Protectorate. Excellent advisors told him the British as yet had no man who could administer justice in the treacherous Okoyong area between the Cross and Calabar rivers. But there was a small redheaded Scottish missionary who could. An imminently practical man, he asked Mary to be his vice-consul in the Okoyong area. She would be in effect the judge who would preside over all native disputes. "Oh no," was her first reaction, but more thought persuaded her that she was indeed the only representative of the British who could be just to the Okoyong. So she took on one more crushing job because no one could do it as well. The gravity of it numbed her, but she knew she would not be sitting behind some high podium in a black robe and white wig. No, her justice would be administered in the savage wilds of Okoyong.

"But administer it, I will!" she promised.

When she disembarked in Duke Town she was presented with a small river steamer, a present of schoolchildren in Scotland. The Efiks and Okoyong marveled at it and called it the "Smoking Canoe." The steamer was a wonderful vessel for spreading the gospel, and once again she seemed following in her hero Livingstone's footsteps. He, too, had his own steamer on the Zambesi River.

But her visit in Duke Town was disturbing, too.

FOURTEEN

Young Charles Morrison was crushed by developments. His health was failing. Mary could not console him. He told her he would soon be going back to Scotland.

"From there, who knows?" he mumbled. "Perhaps to America."

Shaken, Mary returned to Ekenge. There she was never allowed to dwell on her own problems long, for greater human tragedies awaited in her yard. Most Okoyong knew nothing yet of Mary's new official role. They just knew sanctuary could be found with the White Ma. In her yard hid two runaway slaves who had been accused of witchcraft by a chief. Besides those two, a slave woman was hiding from her owner. Mary would not only have to resolve these disputes but now all others in Okoyong, as well.

"In my new role as vice-consul," she informed her friend Eme Ete.

Eme Ete continued to be Mary's greatest ally. Mary owed so much to Chief Edem's clever sister. But sometimes Eme Ete was detained. So the two women worked out a code. If a messenger brought a medicine bottle from Eme Ete it meant, "Be alert for trouble." And Eme Ete approved heartily a new scheme devised by Mary to delay action between warring factions. Mary now sent a runner dashing to the location of the dispute, brandishing a white sheet of paper. On it Mary had scrawled a few simple sentences urging restraint until she arrived. Most important was the red sealing wax and her official stamp.

"This is from the White Ma," the warring clans would agree. "All quarreling must cease until she gets here!"

Once there Mary would seat herself under an umbrella and pull out her bag of needlework. Knitting had a calming influence on the belligerents as well as herself. The Okoyong would argue for hours as she listened and knitted and prayed. Often children gathered around her feet. Occasionally she cooed to a baby in her arms. Sometimes the belligerents, flanked by armed warriors, talked all day, all through the night, and into the next day.

Whenever it was needed Mary defused hot tempers with jokes and reprimands. When it seemed even the disputants were tired of repeating themselves Mary would ask each side to sum up, then render a verdict. It was soon understood her verdict was law. The old ways were over. Mary brought the new ways. The chiefs who had visited Creek Town warned one and all about the great British ships and their giant guns.

"So all must abide by the ruling of the White Ma,"

the chiefs said of the diminutive redheaded missionary.

To seal an agreement the Okoyong often performed a ritual that disgusted Mary. Representatives from both sides clasped hands. A third man cut the backs of their hands with a knife. Onto the flowing blood he sprinkled salt, pepper and corn. The two men chanted an oath, then to Mary's revulsion the two slurped up the horrid gruel. Every time it happened Mary bluntly told the disputants how much she detested this ritual, but she would not stop them. They had to indulge some of their old ways.

"A disgusting ritual for a covenant is better than killing," she told Janie.

Usually the oath, or *mbiam*, taken by Okoyong before testifying in Mary's native court was the one carried out with a human skull and a "truth potion" so foul-smelling Mary insisted it be kept a good distance away when not in use. The witness sprinkled the potion on his tongue, face, arms, and legs. According to their beliefs, if he lied while carrying the potion he would die. One man who took the potion, then denied in front of Mary that he had stolen some plantains, actually did drop dead. There was no native who did not believe he died because he lied under *mbiam*.

Mary believed it herself. "The guilty man's belief was so strong he killed himself with stress," she explained.

Although Mary had great authority among the Okoyong, a few still talked against her. She was just a tiny woman, they protested. Defy her. How could the white men with guns come into the jungle against the Okoyong? But in 1893 the word spread that the white men could indeed do that. Outside Mary's realm, a chief on the Cross River had killed some Ibo traders. The British soldiers came and arrested him. He was tried and hanged!

"Lord have mercy on his soul," said Mary, "and praise God that our Chief Edem has already experienced his change of heart."

Sometimes Mary handed out more justice than a litigant wanted. One day a man named Okpono came to court suing his brother-in-law for a small debt. This irritated Mary greatly because it was legalism at its worst. She knew for a fact Okpono was a rogue who neglected his children and beat his wives with relish, especially the wife, who was the sister of the defendant. On the other hand, the defendant was a decent man who worked hard but was plagued with bad luck.

"How do you plead?" she asked the defendant. "Do you owe Okpono money or not?"

"Guilty," he mumbled sheepishly.

"This court orders you to pay Okpono the money you owe him," said Mary. Then infuriated by the smug look of victory on Okpono's face she added, "And I also order you to give Okpono a good whipping, here and now! Do it thoroughly, too—or I'll fine you."

Mary was not above handing out corporal punishment herself. Back in Old Town she had routed Egbo runners with her umbrella, but she had always wondered how Okoyong warriors would react to physical force. Then one day in Ekenge a drunk barged into her yard with a gun. Hardly thinking, she yanked the weapon out of his hands and gave him a resounding slap in the face. He backed off. After that she had given several Okoyong men a good boxing of the ears. Her use of force at first had not been calculated so much as it had been an expression of utter exasperation. She knew her tiny fists did no more than shock a man. But shock them it certainly did.

Use of corporal punishment crept into her court, too. But this was administered not so much from exasperation, but calculation. On one occasion she had banished a chief from her court because of his obnoxious interruptions. While holding court later Mary was visited by T. D. Maxwell, a British official. Soon after Maxwell arrived, the banished chief appeared. Mary calmly handed the baby she was cuddling to a person standing nearby. She removed her lace shawl and rose from her rocking chair.

"Didn't I tell you not to enter my court again?" she asked the obnoxious chief.

"I came to visit the official, Mr. Maxwell." The chief snorted.

"Nonsense! That's just an excuse."

With that she rushed off to grab him by the back of his neck. She whopped the side of his head and shoved him away. *"Soi, wara do!"* she barked, shooing him off. Mr. Maxwell's mouth gaped. Mary stood, hands on hips, watching the chief and his minions slink off until she was sure they had left the vicinity. Then she returned to her chair, donned her lace shawl, and calmly asked for the baby. After she had finished the proceedings for the day, she chatted with Mr. Maxwell.

When he left later she startled him by saying, "Now you be a good laddie, too."

Some of Mary's cases were horrific: twin killing, murder, esere-bean poisoning. These Mary agonized over. She was determined to render a just decision. She now studied the Bible as never before. It and prayer were the source of her great resolve.

The wisdom of the Bible never failed to awe her. What a gift from God to mankind this great book was! Her reading, usually done at the first light of day before the children or the Okoyong could make demands on her, was intense. No casual reader, she forced herself to reflect deeply and pray over every line. What did a specific verse mean? What did it mean to her in her particular circumstances? Then she jotted her thoughts down on the margin of the page with a fine-point pen.

In her days at Okoyong, even before she began meting out justice, she especially read the Old Testament because she seemed to be living in Old Testament times—before God gave Moses the Ten Commandments. "This occurs at Okoyong every day," she might note. Or, "This could be a chapter of the history of Calabar!" Or "Like the palaver of chiefs at Ekenge."

She poured over Job. She could certainly understand great suffering. "Yes, Job, turn to God, leave it to Him," she wrote in the margin. She also noted, "Your depression will end when you have probed the depths of God," as much for herself as Job.

Only fools were puzzled by God's Word, she came to conclude. And she had to chuckle over that because philosophizing fools were portrayed, too, in Job and other books of the Bible. "Self-centered, arbitrary, hard," she noted. Or, "Much truth but served without love." Yes, she adored the poetry and the wisdom and the guidance in the Old Testament.

Not that she neglected the New Testament. After all, without love—the great message of the New Covenant with the Trinity—life was nothing. "We must know Christ before we can instruct," she wrote. The book of

John gave her much solace. After one passage she scolded herself, "This is why we can't win men; they don't find Christ in us." After another: "Living will reveal; talking proves nothing."

With Chief Edem's change of heart and the efforts of Mary and Eme Ete, how things changed in Ekenge after 1888. Drunkenness was rare now for women, a development that Mary was sure would eventually change the men for the better, too. At one time sinful women boldly roamed the villages, plying their trade; that was virtually unseen now. Raiding villages and capturing people for slaves had ended, too. So had human sacrifice. And the constant turmoil over imagined witchcraft accounting for any death but old age was ending. The gospel had done all that.

Twin murder remained the most intractable atrocity. It was the most secretive, the most difficult to detect. Perhaps the only real progress in that realm of violence was that the mother was not likely to be murdered with Mary in the vicinity. Mary took in twins without fail if she knew about them before they were murdered.

But the Okoyong agonized over twins. "I can't come to the White Ma's now," Chief Edem would moan if he heard she harbored twins. Later he would feel guilty and lavish food on the mission house. His brother Ekpenyong suffered the same way. Even Eme Ete, though tolerating the presence of twins, could not bring herself to hold one. Only Akom, Ekpenyong's wife, could embrace a twin. And of the four only she had accepted Christ.

"The Okoyong are in great turmoil," acknowledged Mary, "but Christ is slowly changing their ways."

Of course the mission house had long been up in Ekenge and the church in Ifako, but there were now also schoolhouses in many villages. Of all Mary's projects the education of the children was the farthest from realized. There were many reasons for that. She was short-handed. She herself had little time to teach because of her other responsibilities. Also, the new ambition she had spurred in the Okoyong worked against schooling. They were people of commerce now. Children had plantains to pick, manioc to boil, palm oil kernels to crush. And it was hard indeed for them to appreciate endless drills in reading and writing. There were virtually no books in their language. There were virtually no occupations that depended on schooling.

"Those days will come, but not right away," Mary told Eme Ete.

In late 1894 Mary united the Okoyong under one authority as it had never been united before. It started with a not unusual case of a slave being blamed for his master's death. But the dispute was in a distant village. The jungle was being lashed by a squall, so Mary sent one of her messages sealed with red wax. But this time the chief of the village defied her. The slave had been hustled off to an even more distant location.

"*Ekem!*" she declared to one and all, "Enough! My patience is at an end. I am tired of chasing fools through the jungle. I am sending for the British troops and the gunboats!"

Mary made sure many villagers heard about this new threat. Even Eme Ete was stunned. Was Mary bluffing? Mary knitted and waited for the threat to spread like wildfire. The result was one of outrage against the chief in the distant village. Was he going to bring the wrath of the British guns against all of Okoyong? It wasn't long before the chief from the distant village appeared at her yard. He was contrite but still wanted to negotiate over the slave. Mary refused to see him. The chief returned to his village, undoubtedly to palaver with his own elders. Mary was sure he was lashed with a lot of heated advice along the way, too. Soon word came back from him.

"The chief says he released the slave," said Eme Ete, "and he wishes the British troops to come in peace, not in war."

Mary was not naive. "Bring the slave to me for safekeeping, and I will tell the British to come in peace."

Mary was grateful that the slave soon appeared. But now she had to produce the British troops from Duke Town, so the Okoyong would know it was no idle threat. It was a great opportunity to unite the Okoyong once and for all under British civility. She asked all chiefs to be in Ekenge for a palaver. On the day of the palaver, at her request, crack British troops bearing the most modern weapons did appear at Ekenge. Then Mary had her palaver with the chiefs. Once again they promised to eradicate human sacrifice, twin killing, and revenge for imagined witchcraft. But this time the chiefs seemed to truly know it was necessary to give up these old ways to keep the British troops out. And Mary, rather than being the harsh judge, was now the alternative to something much worse.

One day not much later Mary said wistfully, "It is an irony that the very ambition King Eyo Honesty and I instilled in the Okoyong chiefs will soon make my works for them at Ekenge and Ifako obsolete."

For the chiefs discovered virgin soil produced better crops of the produce they were beginning to trade. The Okoyong had half-heartedly toiled untold years—perhaps centuries—around Ekenge for simple subsistence. Now, first one family and then another moved from Ekenge to the village of Akpap to find virgin soil. Akpap had the further advantage in being closer to the Cross River, which carried traders back and forth between the coast and the distant outpost of Okofiorong. The Okoyong at Akpap planned to take their produce to the vigorous market already established on the Cross River at Ikunetu.

How much longer can I minister to a shrinking flock? wondered Mary.

When Eme Ete herself left to establish a "farm" near Akpap on virgin soil, Mary was shocked. If Chief Edem decided to go too, the Okoyong would leave Ekenge in droves. They had no intention of being left without a protector. So Mary watched almost mournfully. Not that she had time to mope. Her duties as vice-consul were too demanding. But she had no plans to build anything more in this part of the Okoyong. When would Chief Edem decide to leave Ekenge?

By 1896 Chief Edem still remained in Ekenge, but Akpap was too large for Mary to neglect. She built a two-room house there and began a new ministry. Soon she was spending more time in Akpap than Ekenge.

Suddenly it seemed every village in the Okoyong sent reports of natives being felled by a high fever that lasted about four days, then broke out in a nasty rash that swelled into angry pimples. That wasn't the worst part. The pustules on the victims broke and scabbed over. This was a very dangerous period because the victim either died or recovered, often badly scarred.

"Smallpox," concluded Mary, her heart pounding with dread. "Brought to the Okoyong by the traders."

There was a vaccine of sorts for the disease. Healthy people were inoculated with "mild" forms of smallpox itself. Usually this protected people, but sometimes the inoculation caused them to die. Still, Mary went about inoculating villagers of Akpap. Then word came that Ekenge, neglected these days, was battling the disease like no other village. Mary rushed there. Many of the old chiefs who had helped her change the very soul of the Okoyong were dead already. One was old Ekpenyong. Chief Edem himself was very sick with smallpox. Mary cared for him as best she could, but there was little to do except let the disease run its course. To Mary's grief, the disease killed Chief Edem.

"This is a very great man of the Okoyong we are burying," she consoled Eme Ete, who had come there from her farm.

Mary had few helpers. She fashioned coffins out of wood herself. She even dug graves. Burial itself was special in these horrific days. Mary had turned the mission house into a hospital, and corpses were collecting there. There was nothing she could do about it. She couldn't keep up with the deaths. Eme Ete had gone back to her farm.

Finally it was all too much for Mary. Exhausted, she stumbled along the trail to Akpap, then collapsed in her house. Charles Ovens and another missionary awakened her later. They had come from Calabar to help.

"Go to Ekenge," she sighed.

When the two returned they said Ekenge was a ghost town. Corpses were stacked. Okoyong were even lying dead in the jungle. These natives had fled the villages to no avail.

Mary had never felt so depressed. Yes, she had brought some of these people salvation, but the vast majority did not know Christ. The tragedy and injustice of that overwhelmed her. The death of Ekenge itself depressed her beyond measure. It seemed only yesterday she had arrived there, among the fighting and feuding. Now the jungle would reclaim it as if it had never been. Vanity, vanity. She felt like the disillusioned old sage of Ecclesiastes.

Charles Ovens didn't like the defeat he saw in her eyes and advised her to take a furlough. It had been five years. But how could she leave now? There was so much to do: schooling, church services, medical attention, orphans. And surely the Okoyong would allow no other white person to judge their disputes.

Charles Ovens left determined. "I'll take this to the mission committee."

FIFTEEN

But Mary was not compelled to take a furlough; she now seemed to rule her own world. She toiled on month after month, season after season, year after year. One day as she was writing a necessary dispatch she recorded her surroundings: strangers who had come to see her stood off in the distance, afraid of her twins; four dependent children played around her feet; five village boys were out in the yard, getting a school lesson from Janie; a runaway slave lounged about the yard, waiting for Mary to resolve a dispute with his master; a chief was comforting a young girl with ulcers he brought to Mary for medical treatment; a woman in the yard awaited Mary's solution for her abusive husband; a girl dawdled, expecting her school lesson from Mary; and three others waited for medical treatment.

"Yes, how could I ever find time for a furlough?" she asked the toddlers at her feet.

But Charles Ovens finally returned to Akpap in early

1898. He had returned to build Mary a large mission house. He would be there for some time, maybe an entire year. Mary must take that opportunity to take a furlough, he said. It wasn't a suggestion either, but an order from the mission board. Ovens would administer justice as best he could while she was gone. Mary found havens for as many of her bairns as she could. But she would not leave any of them in jeopardy. So she left for England with Janie, almost grown at sixteen; "Little Mary," five; Alice, three; and Maggie, sixteen months. Mary Slessor herself was a well-worn fifty years old.

"Half a century," she murmured, even more startled to realize she had been in Africa for over twenty years!

She settled first at Joppa with her old friend Mrs. M'Crindle, but it was soon apparent she needed more room for the four children. Generous women of the church found her more spacious lodgings at St. Boswell's. There Mary luxuriated in the hauntingly beautiful Scotland of Sir Walter Scott. His Abbotsford House was nearby, as well as one of his favorite spots to cogitate, Smailholm Tower. The rolling treeless landscape was a microcosm of Scotland, rocks jutting from grass like green velvet.

After Mary was deemed rested, she began to speak in public again. Reporters described her as petite, with a face like tan parchment and straight, parted hair no longer flaming vermilion but rust brown. Her peculiarities were observed, too. She would not cross a street alone. She refused once to cross a pasture because there was a cow grazing in it. She still feared men in audiences. To the Scots it was hard to imagine a more timid woman in all Christendom. Was her famed courage among the most savage people on earth a fiction? An audience in an Edinburgh church found out. Several speeches had been made. An appeal had been made for a collection. As the collection was taken, some in the audience began to fidget in their pews, then whisper, then speak out loud.

"Do you not know these offerings are for the Lord?" boomed Mary, rising with hands on hips. "Is that not an act of worship? Then where is your reverence? The most impoverished convert in Calabar would not be so thoughtless as to chatter during worship!"

Mary's courage came from Christ and was reserved for the larger issues. Offerings certainly triggered a resentment in her. There was a smugness, an indifference about it that irritated her. Yes, it was good that people gave money. But that didn't exactly equate them with the poor widow who gave her last farthing, did it?

And where were the volunteers? To another audience she railed, "If the mission in Calabar fails, it is our failure and not God's. Where are the men and women we need?" Then, referring to one of Britain's military successes, she said, "When Lord Kitchener needed help to vanquish the Sudan, thousands of our brightest were there to help him. But what of the battle for the souls of the heathen? Where are the warriors for the Cross? The banner of the Lord goes begging!"

Her four children seemed like fish out of water. And there was too much to do in Akpap to "spout off" all over Scotland and England. Besides, winter was setting in. So she embarked for Africa after less than a year in Britain. Aboard the steamer she and the children celebrated the birth of the Lord. Once back in Akpap her irritation over the lack of volunteers seemed prophetic. The women helpers who had been promised her at various times, even by the mission board this last time in Scotland, still did not appear. And contrary to the assumption by casual observers that peace in the Okoyong required fewer helpers, peace required more. If Britain expected these people to live by British law, someone must administer it. Mary was swamped now with disputes over trading and property, besides trying to run a mission house, conduct church services, and teach school!

"And where is the ordained missionary who was promised me?" she sputtered.

She grew more exasperated. By means of the Lord using her as an instrument, the Okoyong had been brought into the fold. But where was the follow-up? At times she felt betrayed. Yes, she was the "White Ma," but must she be the mother of thousands? Must she tend to each child separately? It seemed so.

Was her labor in vain? *Certainly not,* she kept reminding herself. Human sacrifice among the Okoyong had stopped. Drunkenness and prostitution were much diminished. Many twins were rescued, and their mothers were rarely murdered now.

But could she continue with so little help? Past fifty now, her health began to fail.

Part of the problem was the elaborate European style mission house Charles Ovens had built in Akpap. It didn't stay dry the way native mud houses did. Mary had long suspected native huts properly floored and ventilated were excellent shelter, and they could be built for so little money. The only extravagances she really approved of were cement floors and proper windows and doors.

The moisture in the new mission house caused an onset of arthritis. Insomnia lent its crippling effect, too. Fatigue bred doubts. She couldn't remember being in such a state of misery and self-doubt since her youth when her drunken father terrorized the household. Not long after her return to Akpap she was bedridden for three months.

In the tropics one never knew if prolonged illness would end in death or not. But every day she thanked God that she had the hope of a Christian. What did wretches without Christ do for comfort? She shuddered to think about it. Then she began to worry about her children. What would happen to them if she passed on? To think of them, especially her "daughters," sinking back into depravity made her sicker yet. So she resolved that if the mission board ever turned her out she would settle in the tiniest hut to be near her children. She would never leave Africa. Hadn't Livingstone done the same? Retirement in England or Scotland with plum pudding? Unthinkable. To subsist in Africa on manioc and fetid river water was infinitely better.

On December 21, 1899, Janie at seventeen wed Akibo Eyo in a Christian ceremony. Mary was able to officiate because marriage in the United Presbyterian Church of Scotland was not a sacrament. Janie and her husband went to live with Eme Ete on her farm.

Mary became more depressed. Janie was so dear to her. And such a great help to her. Official duties, including Mary's role as British vice-consul, seemed ever more crushing. Even housework weighed on her. As she often reflected, in Africa the woman must be butcher, baker, nurse, and washerwoman. At the moment of Janie's departure Mary Slessor, the "White Ma," tended three toddlers and nine babies!

Occasionally she was visited by other missionaries, the young ones gawking at her as if they were witnessing a legend. One confessed to Mary, "In Duke Town it is difficult for me to know what to do."

"You don't have to *do* anything, lassie!" snapped Mary. "First, you must *be*. The doing will follow."

Mary had become gruff. She knew that. After a stinging rebuke like that one, she followed with motherly tenderness. She truly wanted to inspire young missionaries. It was just hard for her to tolerate muddled thinking, especially when the Bible gave such clear instructions. Maybe that was why she was so biting. Weren't these youngsters reading the Bible? Her sharpness destroyed visitors' notions they were being treated to a lovable old "character," although she had to admit any European woman walking around without hat or shoes would surely be labeled a character. Mary refused to boil water or use mosquito netting besides. Well, this is what she had become to serve Christ. Would she carry on her crushing duties in Akpap to her last breath, becoming ever more depressed and eccentric?

"If it is Your will, Lord," she wearily noted.

To her amazement a new challenge grew in her heart. West of Okoyong, between the Cross River and the Niger River was territory with a history of horrifying tyranny. Refugees from there often confided in Mary. Tyranny there had not been vigilante terror like the Egbo runners or warrior tyranny like that in Okoyong—but tyranny by an elite priesthood called the Aros, not the least of their vile sins being slavery and cannibalism. The remarkable thing about the Aros was that they were a small tribe within many thousands—perhaps millions—of Ibos and about as many Ibibios. The Aros had controlled the masses by mystical mumbo-jumbo called the Long Juju. Thousands of innocents made pilgrimages to the Aro priests' center at Arochuku, where the poor souls were enslaved or eaten! It was new High Commissioner Ralph Moors who decided this vilest of sects must be quashed. Since 1900 the territory under British domination had expanded inland, the colony now called Protectorate of Southern Nigeria. To emphasize the British claim on this new territory, a military expedition crushed the Aros. But now that country was in chaos.

"Could I dare take on a new challenge?" Mary asked herself in January of 1903, and her depression evaporated.

As incredible as anything Mary had ever done, she took her older children and journeyed up the Cross River to Itu, once a notorious slave market run by the Aros. From there she traveled up Enyong Creek, which drained the highlands of the Aros, Ibos, and Ibibios to the west.

She talked to the old chiefs. They very much wanted to learn of these new things. The population along Enyong Creek was far denser than that of the Okoyong or even that around Duke Town and Creek Town. Within just three miles of Arochuku were sixteen villages larger than Creek Town! How could people so numerous and starving for the truth—that could only be revealed by the gospel—be ignored?

I must not neglect them, resolved Mary, and she felt twenty years younger.

So she returned to Akpap and demanded a replacement. That spring Miss Wright arrived in Akpap. Well pleased with the newcomer's competence, Mary decided to leave Akpap for Itu as soon as practical. She even ventured up Enyong Creek again in June, getting a mission house under way in Itu and starting a school in the village of Amasu. Never had it been so easy to enlist native help. But she soon returned to Akpap.

"I can't miss this very important anniversary," she told Miss Wright.

On August 4, 1903, it was difficult for Mary to believe she had been in Okoyong fifteen years. But was that any harder to believe than the fact that she had been in Africa twenty-seven years? To honor her Okoyong anniversary, Duke Town sent Reverend Weir to Akpap to conduct the first baptisms and the first holy communion ever held in the Okoyong. That was how little support Mary had received from the mission board, she reflected sadly. Still, hadn't Christ used her to bring the entire region under civil law? So perhaps the Lord approved of the board's neglect. On this fifteenth anniversary, the Okoyong of Akpap were also chartering a native church.

"Okoyong is now in the hands of those I converted," she told them. To herself she gloried, *And now I am truly free to move on.*

By January 1904 she had resigned as vice-consul; she had received from the mission committee a six-month leave to be an itinerant along Enyong Creek. This she said would replace her normal furlough, for she had no desire to ever return to Britain again. The committee gave her its blessing but told her it could spare no money for any projects she might initiate. At the age of fifty-five she departed for Itu, where she already had a congregation of several hundred eager babes in Christ. Still, the mission house there, though large and well-constructed, was unfinished. So a rejuvenated Mary poured a cement floor and whitewashed the walls—with the help of Janie, who had left her husband because he could not live as a Christian.

All along Enyong Creek Mary discovered an eagerness for learning she had never seen before. Mary first made it clear to the chiefs that there could be no teaching without Christ. Chiefs in Arochuku declared they were ready for a teacher. So did the village of Akani Obio. The chief there wanted a church so desperately he chopped down their sacred Juju tree to build it. Within months churches were started at Oko, Odot, and Asang.

Christianity bloomed so rapidly among the Ibos and Ibibios the mission committee was happy to extend her furlough from Akpap. They relented on financial aid, too. They not only helped with the mission house at Itu but built a medical facility there, run by Dr. Robertson, a physician from Cape Town. Mary was stunned by the name given the facility.

" 'Mary Slessor Mission Hospital'!" she gasped. "All I can do is look up at the heavens and say, 'O Lord, let me live in You and be worthy of this honor.' "

South of Enyong Creek was the land of the Ibibios. The British were opening up this region at a lightning pace, building roads everywhere. Mary had never seen anything like it. Where once natives trod gladed jungle paths scarcely wide enough to allow one walker to pass another there now stretched smooth dirt roads wide enough for "horseless carriage" contraptions called automobiles. There was even talk of building a railroad north from Port Harcourt to Enugu to tap the coal deposits there.

Because of the onslaught of European culture Mary knew the missionaries had to bring Christ to the Ibibios as quickly as possible. So she went south from Enyong Creek to the village of Ikotobong, where she and a young Efik coworker started a school and a congregation. The youth was a natural teacher, soon attracting fifty children.

Encouraged by half-serious British soldiers, Mary took to riding a bicycle up and down the newly constructed roads. Gliding along like that was much easier on her now chronically arthritic joints than stumbling over roots on jungle paths.

She was never more determined. "My furlough will end April 1906," she told her coworkers. "If the mission committee says I must return to Akpap, as beloved to me as that village is, for the first time ever I feel their directions to me are not ordained by God." She reflected how she had served many years in Creek Town, all the while waiting to go to Okoyong. "No, this time I will be compelled to ignore their orders. My work among the Ibos and Ibibios must continue—even if I must quit the mission!"

But Mary need not have worried. The mission fully backed her efforts with money and manpower. Missionary John Rankin was appointed to manage the

Ibo activity, centered mainly in Itu and Arochuku. This freed Mary to minister solely among the Ibibios.

British authorities could not ignore her presence. She was soon contacted to begin working among the Ibibios as a judge over a native court, much as she had at Okoyong. She accepted the position, starting in Ikotobong in May 1906. Once again Mary had all disputants take *mbiam*, the native oath. Fear of its power made Ibibios amazingly honest, even incriminating themselves. She was tough, especially with men who abused women.

"I find you guilty!" she told a man who had stolen from a girl in the market. "One month hard labor!"

"Guilty!" she informed another man, who had seized a girl and held her captive for two weeks. "Six months hard labor!" Six months was the longest sentence she could give under her jurisdiction.

Many men were not technically guilty. According to native law men could beat their wives to a certain point with complete impunity. But Mary, even though she could not "legally" punish these brutes, did not hesitate to rap such men on the sides of their heads with her umbrella. Anyone else in her court, whether charged with a crime or not, who disrupted the proceedings could expect the same treatment. More than one chief who repeated himself once too often found his ear stinging from a blow!

She could level men with words, too, for Mary knew all the nuances of the language. She scalded many a man with sarcasm.

Not all the proceedings were grim. Once all the people inside the court scrambled outside to gawk at an automobile chug-chugging by. And she often softened her justice. If the guilty were obviously penniless, Mary would sternly lecture them and put them to work at the mission for a while.

"No one seems to resent it," she explained.

Her judicial work did not keep her from normal mission activity or even from inventing new projects. To everyone's astonishment she announced she planned to build a rest home for missionaries on Enyong Creek in country so wild that after a rain the dirt road there was covered with leopard tracks. Skeptics were silenced when she acquired the parcel of land and initiated the clearing of it. Giving her ever more support, the mission committee decided to staff her mission house in Ikotobong with women volunteers.

Mary was ever quick to seize opportunities. "I'm moving my court to the village of Use."

Never had success come so fast—but then suddenly Mary was leveled.

SIXTEEN

Mary's health, which for years had fluctuated from usually adequate to occasionally bedridden, disintegrated under extreme arthritis. In her new village of Use she was able to walk no more than few steps at a time. She was still able to conduct court, but for any other activity she had to have helpers carry her around.

The doctor at the mission hospital in Itu put his foot down. "Go back to Scotland and rest, or you will collapse, perhaps permanently."

So Mary left Africa in May 1907. This time she took only one child with her: six-year-old Dan. A few weeks later she was rolling into Edinburgh on the train, to be met by her old friend Mrs. M'Crindle. The concern in her friend's eyes told her how much she had aged in nine years. Mary didn't mind having skin like an accordion or hair gloomy gray. Those were vanities. But being crippled depressed her.

How can I carry on my work for the Lord? she asked herself.

Mary rested in St. Boswell's again. She visited her old haunts in Dundee, pleased to see the great two-mile rail bridge across the Tay rebuilt. Scots persevered to be sure. The boy Dan fell in love with Scotland. Mary began to recover. She even tried bicycling. But then she received a well-intentioned letter from Africa that hinted Janie was in bad company. Mary could not relax after that. She gave a few obligatory speeches, reluctantly accepted an avalanche of praise, then shocked everyone by booking passage on an October voyage to Africa. Her leave was going to last a mere five months.

All the way back she prayed. "Lord have mercy on Janie."

Once in Duke Town she had to find out about Janie right away. The letter was wrong, she was reassured. Janie was all right. Mary prayed her thanks to God and returned to the Ibibios at the village of Use. Besides her normal duties as judge and missionary she began new projects. Her settlement for abandoned girls started with a modest three huts. The girls were encouraged to develop simple crafts like making baskets and weaving mats. To help her mission Mary planted pineapples, bananas, mangoes, pawpaws, plantains, avocados, and guavas. She pushed herself hard, tired and crippled though she was. Miss Peacock and the other woman who ran the mission at nearby Ikotobong began looking in on her frequently.

By 1909 Mary's health worsened with the onset of boils. Still she expanded her activity. Once again it was because refugees told her of an extremely degraded part of the wilderness. Far west on the upper reaches of the Enyong Creek was the town of Ikpe, they said, wallowing in depravity. A tiny band of people there were trying to be Christians.

Of course Mary had to go there. It was so important to her she resigned her judicial position. Her doctors demanded she slow down. What about her health? What about the hippos that terrorized the fifty miles of swollen river that had to be traveled to reach Ikpe? Hippos looked slow and clumsy—even funny to ignorant Europeans—but they killed many Africans every year. The bulls were so volatile they didn't hesitate to ram their enormous bulk into canoes. A bite from a hippo tusk could go right through a human body—and often did.

"I've encountered hippos before." Mary shrugged, remembering once slamming an oversized pot lid into the gaping jaws of a hippo.

Mary traveled two days by boat to reach Ikpe. She discovered everything about Ikpe had been understated. The town was much larger than she expected. The market was enormous, serving several trade routes. The wickedness was extreme. Woman were especially mistreated, bought and sold like livestock. They were naked except for beads. Children were foul-mouthed thieves. Could Mary ignore such festering evil?

She found the tiny group trying to be Christians. "Yes, I most certainly will help you build a church," she told them.

Mary began traveling Enyong Creek back and forth from Ikpe to Use. Often she was slowed to a crawl by arthritis, but to her this new activity was "real life." Retiring was "death." Many mornings she forced herself to rise by thinking of the fledgling Christians in Ikpe trying to hold a Sunday church service. Not one of the poor babes in Christ could read. Oh, why weren't there more missionaries? And off she would go. Two days later her helpers in Ikpe would lift her stiff body out of the canoe. Besides conducting church services, sometimes she had to be carried to the market to prevent bloodshed. On the return trip from Ikpe she often hugged a motherless baby to her breast.

Yes, this is the real life, she reassured herself.

Once in the summer of 1911 she returned to find her Use house tattered from one of the vicious line squalls they called a "tornado." She immediately pitched in to repair the damage. Her health failed her as never before. She was dizzy, breathless, sweating. Did she now have heart trouble? She fell in bed with a fever, shaken. Her money was so low at times she had trouble buying groceries. So she wasn't eating well either. This worsened her health more.

Miss Peacock had Dr. Hitchcock come from the mission hospital in Uti to examine her.

"Overworked and undernourished," fumed the doctor. "If you weren't so stubborn, you would have been dead long ago. Now don't leave that bed unless I give you permission. And eat meat twice a day."

"I don't eat meat, doctor."

Dr. Hitchcock must have suspected she didn't eat meat because she could not afford any. Before he returned to Uti he had chickens sent to Mary's house. But her health didn't improve. Soon the doctor had her at Uti in a hospital room.

"Life in a hospital bed isn't living at all," she complained to the doctor.

Men from Ikpe visited. "When are you coming back?" they asked her.

"Seven weeks from now at the earliest," snapped the doctor, who overhead the question.

After the doctor left Mary said, "I may run up to Ikpe a bit sooner than that, laddies."

But for once Mary did not bounce back. The hospital was "death" to her and she brooded. Old friends had passed away, like James Logie back in Scotland. Then there was Charles Morrison, the only man she thought she loved. His fate was very disturbing. He had gone to America to seek seclusion and write, living as a hermit in the woods like the American writer Henry Thoreau. But fire consumed his cabin and all his years of writing. Did it crush him? Charles Morrison died shortly after that. So young, too. Why?

"In my 'real life' I don't have time to brood," said Mary.

She decided she must leave, sick or not. Near the end of 1911 she fled the hospital. In Ikpe she celebrated the birth of Christ. Janie, now teaching several hundred Ibibios in Nkanga, came to celebrate, too. But the "real life" did not rejuvenate Mary this time. She scarcely had one hour of real energy during a day now. A gift from well-informed friends in Scotland helped her. It was a "Cape cart," in which she sat upright as two youngsters wheeled her around.

"O Lord, even this is too much for me," she admitted.

Soon her activity was limited to being carried to church meetings and teaching children while slumped in a chair on the verandah. But still she pushed herself. The mission committee was very worried about her now. Was she intent on working herself to death? Didn't she know how important she was to everyone in Africa? She must come to Duke Town at once and discuss the matter of a furlough.

"It's too late in the year to take a furlough in Scotland," she countered, "I can't endure a northern winter anymore."

"Then you must go to the Canary Islands to rest."

"What an extravagance!"

The Canary Islands were lavish indeed to a woman who some days had to sell a book or two to buy groceries, to a woman who at times had set out on trips with no more provisions than two ears of corn. But the mission and its medical staff compelled her to go. To appease her they let Janie accompany her. The trip required two weeks to the islands, one month on Grand Canary, and two weeks back to Calabar. It was the off season and the hotel staff doted on her. Often she relaxed atop a hill in back of the hotel with Janie, bathed in sunshine and sea breeze. She knitted and read her Bible. The hotel staff brought lunch and tea to the hilltop.

"I can't remember ever being so spoiled," she admitted.

Amazingly, at sixty-four she regained her health. When she returned to Duke Town, the mission and the medical staff praised her recovery, assuring her she had many good years left—if she followed medical instructions. She returned to Use with a list of instructions and a supply of medicine.

She was able to minister to Ikpe again, too, because a government car, which had to go regularly to Ikot

Ekpene near Ikpe, let her ride along. The work at Ikpe made the same demands as Use for teaching, healing, and preaching. But as a young mission it also demanded whitewashing, plastering, cementing, and building. And Mary helped.

"It's a bonny thing for me the doctors don't know what it's like in Ikpe," she reflected.

In July 1913 Mary visited Akpap for the first time in eight years. To her embarrassment it became an occasion heralded throughout the Okoyong. Hundreds of natives flooded in. The two women missionaries who now ran the mission had almost finished a large church. They used the great influx of visitors as an opportunity to dedicate their new church. Four hundred attended the first service. Mary was astonished to see one in attendance.

"Eme Ete!" exclaimed Mary.

The huge woman had aged like Mary. Eme Ete still practiced heathen ways, like many who attended the service just to honor Mary. It was such an irony that this pagan woman had helped Mary overcome the old ways of the Okoyong. For Eme Ete still sacrificed food and blood to her fiercesome gods. She still could not bring herself to touch twins.

Failure to convert Eme Ete was one of Mary's greatest disappointments. Mary agonized over her salvation. It certainly appeared Eme Ete's remaining days on earth were as few as Mary's.

"Can God forget how Eme Ete helped me in those savage days?" Mary inquired of a friend. "I can't even imagine winning Okoyong without her." But Mary had to admit sadly, "Eme Ete made a foolhardy choice. . . ."

Back in Use, Mary received a document asking that

she accept membership into an organization called the Order of the Hospital of St. John of Jerusalem. She was baffled. What did this request mean? Why would she be chosen? Most of all, why accept? She desired no baubles for serving Christ. Still she accepted.

"That should put an end to the whole affair," she grumbled.

Weeks later she received a letter requesting that she come to Calabar to receive her decoration. She would get no peace until the ordeal was over, she reasoned. Days later a government launch arrived to take her to Calabar. At Duke Town she stayed at Mission Hill. She wore her best cotton dress from her meager wardrobe. She added an unaccustomed straw hat and footwear that was more sandals than shoes. On Government Hill she visited the barracks of soldiers and later was their guest at a cricket match. She approved of all games, because to her they were a healthy substitute for the mortal combat she had witnessed all too often. She began to relax. On Sunday after church service she lectured the students on Mission Hill. This visit wasn't so terrible after all.

Of course I should be working, but what choice do I have? she asked herself.

Finally, came a banquet Monday night. It was held in the Goldie Memorial Hall. It seemed every government official was there. So were all the missionaries. As were all students, including the girls of the Edgerley Memorial School and the boys of the Waddell Training Institute.

Like so much in Calabar the origins of the Waddell Institute were linked to Mary. Back in 1891, while furloughed in Scotland, she had fought prevailing opinion that Africans were intractable in their backwardness with a long, factual letter to the *Missionary Record*. "Teach the Africans trades!" she urged. Her voice had been too strong, too sensible to ignore.

This night, at the banquet, tributes to her long service began.

Oh no, she moaned to herself. She buried her face in her hands. She could not look the world in the face again until all this talk was over.

Finally Mary had to relent and stand while a black bow was pinned on her left shoulder. From it hung the silver Maltese Cross with lions on the ends of one arm and unicorns on the ends of the other. It was explained the honor was for those who had performed great things for the faith. Sir Frederick Lugard, the governor-general of the newly formed Colony of Nigeria, had recommended her. His Majesty King George V had personally sanctioned it.

Then Mary spoke, "If this is my crown to take to glory land, I will lay it at the Master's feet."

Then in Efik she addressed the children: They should obey their government not only because the Bible commands it, but because at heart this government was sympathetic to Christian work. The medal proved it, though it could just as well have been awarded to any other missionary in Africa.

Then she spoke in English to the others. She didn't know why she was honored. Others deserved it more. Besides, everything she had done was possible only because the Master had gone before. And she enunciated the stance that she would maintain from that day forward. "This medal is a token of appreciation to all the missionaries in Nigeria," she asserted.

She rushed back to her "real life." How happy she was to have all the fuss over with. But developments at Ikpe worried her.

SEVENTEEN

At Ikpe a small core accepted Christ but the rest were as resistant to Christ as any she had encountered. A few chiefs actively opposed Mary's efforts, intimidating all those who wanted to participate, especially girls. Mary had always felt the girls led the way to total acceptance of the new ways. Without them, the battle was a hundred times harder. If only she could get the chiefs to back off. Finally she managed to arrange a council of chiefs.

Mary told the chiefs, "I agree any who break your ordinary laws should be punished. But I respectfully ask the chiefs to not punish anyone who worships our God, nor should they be forced to worship idols." She asked for nothing less than religious freedom.

The chiefs conferred and finally one of them answered, "We will agree to your request, but we ourselves will not join the confusions of your church!"

So Mary's persistence succeeded in freeing the girls

to attend church. But the chiefs would not let the girls learn how to read and write. Even the boys who attended school were made to tend an infant while they were there, so it was "not a total waste of time." Eventually a few chiefs let their daughters, babes in tow, attend school too—if they received a nice dress from the mission. Mary was happy to oblige. She had always been fortunate in getting clothing from England and Scotland, so she could dress her children. But if any native—man, woman, or child—overdid it and became too "European," Mary would rebuke them in a flash.

Mary still had to deal with twin murder, too. Once she had heard Ibos and Ibibios did not murder twins, but it was obvious that they did. So again she took in twins that had not been killed but abandoned. Even then, she had to watch carefully so some zealot who thought they were children of the devil did not steal them away. Once she and Janie decided to press a mother into keeping her one surviving twin at home. Janie had to virtually live with the mother and guard the baby. For ten weeks Janie persisted, then returned to the mission house. When she went back to check on the child four days later she saw it had not eaten in all that time. Janie rushed it back to the mission.

"Oh no!" cried Mary. "The poor baby has death written on its face."

The baby died. Such tragedies shrouded Mary in gloom. In her thirty-seven years in Africa Mary had brought many thousands from barbarism to a civilized level of paganism, but she had converted only a few hundred to Christianity. Why had God denied his mercy, his grace? For Saint Paul made it clear in the letter to the

Romans the truth of the gospel was "according to the election of grace," not "works," and the rest are "blinded." It was a mystery hard to accept, but Mary did accept it. She was nothing. She followed her Master.

Christmas of 1913 Mary was in Use for the dedication of their new church building. It was mud walled and modest in size, which pleased her. Huge, ornamented church buildings alienated the chiefs, she believed. Besides, the church was the people, and in Mary's mind the large turnout of people was far more impressive than any building. But she overtaxed herself celebrating and was not able to get out of bed for several days. Visitors from Duke Town urged her to go back there with them to recuperate. But Mary remembered the great fuss over her Maltese Cross, and she thought of all the special attention she might get.

"I must stay here," she told them.

From looks full of pity Mary knew everyone thought she was on her deathbed. Yet she arose and began working again in early 1914. She didn't putter around the mission house, either. Mary hopped a ride in a government car and launched a new effort south of Ikpe at Odoro! Even though she had to be wheeled about again in the Cape cart, she harangued local chiefs until she got a school started. Now, with continued attention to Ikpe and Use too, she served three localities.

"If only there were more soldiers in Christ!" she cried. "We British have the privilege of giving Christ to all these lost souls, and it's as if we said to Him, 'No. Perhaps another time.'"

Her mission society had only about as many volunteers in Nigeria now as it had when she first arrived thirty-eight years before. Often she reflected on this with despair. The greatest irony to Mary was the absence of women volunteers. They not only won natives over more quickly, because the natives did not suspect them of being British agents, but Mary knew many thousands of women were whiling away their lives in Britain, bored with silly fashions and superficial amusements. Vanity of vanities. Where were these women? If only they would donate a few months of their wasted time.

"How can I ever justify not working as recklessly as I do?" she asked defensively.

At Odoro she supervised the building of a mission house. She had to sit for hours in the summer sun. Her health held up by sheer willpower. But then in August 1914 the world overwhelmed her. War erupted in Europe. Britain was involved. From what Mary could find out from local British officials, the war began as a local skirmish between Austria-Hungary and Serbia. But various alliances snowballed the skirmish into a European war, which soon would be a world war, the first in the history of mankind. It seemed certain that twenty or so nations, including Britain, France, Russia, Italy, and America, would battle an alliance of Germany, Austria-Hungary, Turkey, and Bulgaria.

"At least Britain was not the aggressor who started this abomination," grumped Mary.

"Will the war come to Africa?" asked Janie.

"We must pray to God that it doesn't," answered Mary. She well knew Britain's Colony of Nigeria shared its eastern border with the Cameroons, a German colony. "There could be fighting right in the Okoyong!"

Horrifying news trickled in. On the twenty-ninth

of August the mounted infantry of the Nigerian Regiment overwhelmed the German post of Tepe in the Cameroons. At the same time they were also attacking the German river port of Garua on the Benue. But the very next day at Garua the Nigerians were defeated in a counterattack. In the south at Nsanakang a hundred Nigerian soldiers were killed in an attack.

There was a lull. "It means nothing," Mary admitted to herself. "This is just the beginning."

She had never felt so weak, so helpless, so depressed, in all her days. Here she had tried for nearly forty years to bring Africans the best her culture had to offer, and it might all be negated by the onset of the worst her culture had to offer. She felt like Job. Only praying and reading her Bible gave her any comfort.

On September 27 the conflagration began again. British ships shelled the Cameroon port of Duala, and Nigerian soldiers stormed ashore with soldiers from French colonies. By Christmas they captured Buea, the capital of Cameroon. It seemed Nigeria was now safe from invaders. In a sense the war was over for the marketplaces along the Cross River and Enyong Creek. There was a lot of local pride in the conquest. Native Nigerians, bearing modern arms, had carried the day.

"So we have now taught the Africans how to kill each other with modern weapons," noted Mary wearily. "Those same weapons can be turned on us."

Two Englishmen Mary knew personally were drowned in the assault on Cameroon. She fought the hatred building inside her against the Germans. But was she not human? She wanted her countrymen safe. So the war in Europe weighed very heavily on her. Was Britain

200

safe? She talked often to British officials in the area. Speculation was endless. Soldiers could float around in the skies now in great dirigibles; they could drop bombs from the heights. Would the Germans launch an armada of "bombers" over Britain? And who would win the terrible war that raged across the trenches in France?

Mary tried to buoy those around her. "We are not the aggressors. We have no lust for conquest. Take solace in that. Remember, God's purpose will not be thwarted by warmongers. Not pharaohs, not Greeks, not Romans, not Huns—and definitely not Germans!"

On Christmas of 1914 she hoped the war-weary world—as never before—felt a profound sense of what Christ meant in His coming. She prayed that in all the homes with empty chairs the people would let Christ fill that chair. Perhaps all those who had spurned Him in prosperity would welcome Him in desperation. "Oh please know," she prayed for the mourning and the fearful, "that He is the Resurrection and the Life; he that believes in Him shall never die."

Her health continued to deteriorate. At sixty-six Mary was now ancient for a white person in the tropics. On New Year's Day of 1915 Miss Peacock and her assistant came to her at Use to celebrate with plum pudding. Mary told how some of the children ran around in church but she didn't reprimand them. The babies should be in God's house, too. She was mellow now. She told her visitors she had recently gone through all her old letters and destroyed many.

"There was little time for softness in those ancient days at Okoyong," she told her friends. *Or even more ancient days at Old Town,* she could have added.

In her failing strength she found herself now writing mothers back in England and Scotland to comfort them. Yes, their sons were in the armed forces, Mary admitted, but in God's governance no precious thing is ever lost. The sons had to do their duty as they saw fit. She wrote friends she would be returning to England and Scotland in March. Her previous furlough had restored her health. And she was much in need of another.

In one letter she admitted she might not live until March.

EIGHTEEN

O n Sunday the tenth of January Mary conducted church services, although she had a fever. The exertion depleted her. She collapsed on the iron cot in her bedroom. Monday she suffered diarrhea and vomiting. Anyone knew this was a lethal combination to people who were already feeble. Her helpers rushed to get Miss Peacock. She in turn sped a messenger to the mission hospital at Itu. By late afternoon Dr. Robertson arrived at Use. He managed to stop the diarrhea and vomiting with medicine. He iced her to try to bring the fever down. Mary was in much pain. She expelled great sighs as they tried to make her comfortable—with no success.

"Ice," she croaked. Her throat was sand.

The doctor put ice on her tongue. A great coolness swept her body. Mary collected her thoughts. Was there anything that needed to be conveyed to Miss Peacock about Mary's effects? She was too weak to laugh at the pompous note in that thought. Except for worn hand-me-down clothing and meager bedroom furnishings, Mary's worldly possessions were her mother's tiny wedding ring, two Bibles, a hymnbook, a watch, a compass, a fountain pen, and a handful of costume jewelry. That paucity was just as it should be.

She fell asleep. When she awoke the next morning the doctor was gone. Miss Peacock was at her side. Flulike pain seared Mary's skin. Her bones ached. No position relieved her of torment. She was restless in trying to find comfort, yet so weak. And the pain nagged at her. She groaned and helping hands anxiously shifted her around. Finally the hands hurt too much. They were unwelcome. Mary could take no more.

"O God, let me go!" she screeched weakly in Efik.

After that she seemed to think tiny thoughts engulfed in pain, a long nightmare that would never end. Or was it one interminable second?

Sobbing reached her ears. Were some of her dearest in the room? Yes, she began to recognize voices. She must somehow think through the pain. Of course, ever-faithful Janie was there—O Lord, could she be thirty-two years old and the adoptive mother of Dan, thirteen? Married Annie had come from Ikotobong. Mary's two unmarried scholars—Alice, nineteen, and Maggie, seventeen—voiced their sorrow. Whitie, her most recent "daughter," was undoubtedly there, intimidated into silence by her elders. Only "Little Mary," now twenty-one and living fifty miles distant in Ikot Ekpene—seemed to be missing. Oh well, the sobbing made Mary feel truly *eka kpukpru owo*, "everybody's mother."

A rooster crowed. Was Wednesday dawning?

Someone whispered with alarm it was not morning at all, it was pitch black outside. Someone else blurted that surely meant the angel of death was coming.

Well, come then, thought Mary. *Good-bye, sweet babies, until we meet again.*

The pain would soon be gone. Her remains would be interred on Mission Hill above Duke Town. But Mary herself was surely going on to paradise. She was never so sure as now, this January 13, 1915. Oh, how she longed to rest her weary bones in the open arms of her Master.